CIVIL WAR BREECH LOADING RIFLES

*A survey of the
innovative Infantry arms
of the
American Civil War.*

BY

John D. McAulay

ANDREW MOWBRAY INC./*Publishers* • P.O. Box 460, Lincoln, Rhode Island USA

LIBRARY OF CONGRESS
CATALOG CARD NO.: 87-060724
    John D. McAulay
      Civil War Breech Loading Rifles
    Lincoln, RI: ANDREW MOWBRAY INCORPORATED — *PUBLISHERS*
    pp. 128

ISBN: 0-917218-29-9

©1987 by John D. McAulay

Second Printing — February, 1991

Printed in the United States of America

*This book is dedicated
to my sisters,
Ann and Jill.*

ACKNOWLEDGEMENTS

In the undertaking of this book, I am greatly indebted to the following individuals for their help in making this book a reality:

Mr. Roy Marcot, the authority on the Spencer Repeating Rifles who provided much useful information on these firearms; Mr. H. Michael Madus, Assistant Curator of History at the Milwaukee Public Museum who provided photographs from the Museum collection and also considerable information on the Ballard rifles; Mr. Norm Flayderman who provided helpful information from his catalogs on the Springfield Joslyn Rifle; Mrs. Betty Skyles for her help in obtaining the post Civil War Naval Ordnance records at the various naval yards as of December 1, 1866; Mr. Stu Vogt for his helpful assistance with Colonel's Berdan's U.S. Sharpshooters; Mr. Mike Musick of the Army and Old Navy Branch of the National Archives for his considerable help in locating vast amounts of ordnance records stored at the Archives; Mr. Herb Peck, Jr., who graciously provided photographs of Civil War tintypes and ambrotypes from his collection; Ms. Donna Tedeschi for her many hours of photographing the author's collection of breechloading rifles which appear in this work; the late Mr. Ralph Arnold for his kindness in allowing the author to use photographs of the Jenks rifles from his collection; Mr. George D. Moller for photographs of the Model 1855 Joslyn rifle from his collection; and finally special thanks to my sister, Mrs. Jill Hedley, and Mrs. Angelea Torres for typing the manuscript.

FOREWORD

Upon completion of *Carbines of the Civil War 1861-1865,* I felt there was a need for a similar study of the breech loading rifles available for use by the United States Army and Navy during the Civil War. This book was, therefore, undertaken to study both those firearms purchased during the conflict by the Federal Government and the various states; and those breech loaders manufacturerd prior to the war but available for use.

The reader will find within these covers the actual serial numbers of a number of Sharps rifles used by Berdan's Sharpshooters; a newspaper account of Wilder's Brigade's use of their new seven shot repeating Spencer rifles at Hoover Gap, Tennessee on June 24, 1863; the number of Spencer rifles used by Custer's Michigan Cavalry at Gettysburg; the first mass produced breech loading rifle manufactured at the Springfield Armory was the Springfield Joslyn rifle; James Durell Greene, the inventor of the first bolt action rifle purchased by the government, led the 17th U.S. Infantry at Gettysburg; and much more.

While the breech loading rifle was not purchased in vast quantities — only about thirty-five thousand were obtained during the war — it is hoped that the student and collector of these interesting firearms will come to more greatly appreicate their use by the troops to whom they were issued.

JOHN D. McAULAY

TABLE OF CONTENTS

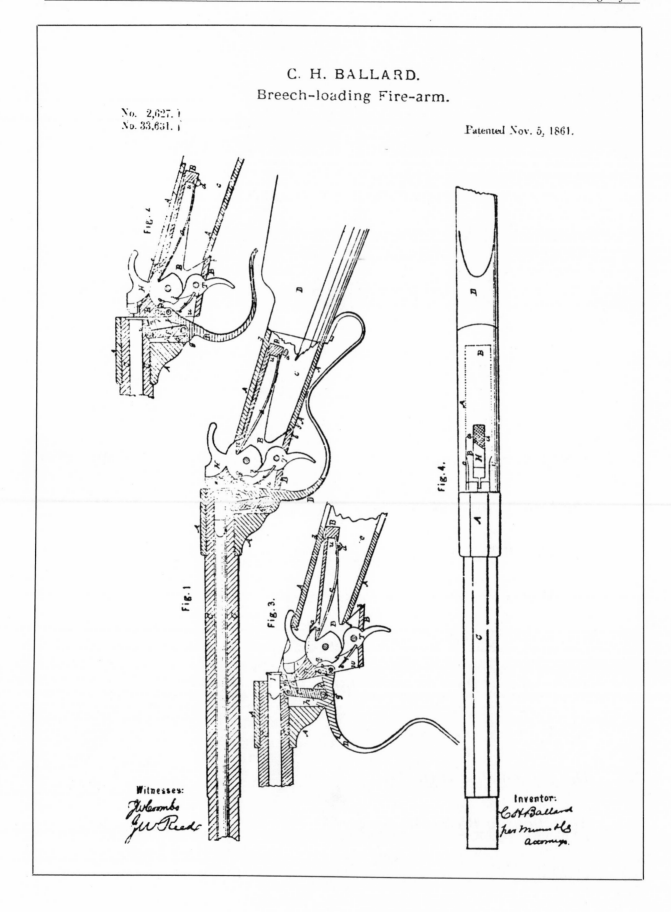

C. H. BALLARD.
Breech-loading Fire-arm.

No. 2,627.
No. 33,631.

Patented Nov. 5, 1861.

Fig. 4.

Fig. 1.

Fig. 3.

Fig. 4.

Witnesses:

Inventor:

THE BALLARD RIFLE

The smallest Ordnance Department procurement for breech-loading rifles during the Civil War was the purchase of thirty-five (35) Ballard rifles in 1863.

The inventor of these single shot rimfire cartridge rifles was Charles Henry Ballard of Worcester, Massachusetts. Charles Ballard was born in 1822 at Brattleboro, Massachusetts. In 1850, he was employed by Ball & Rice, the manufacturers of woodworking machinery. In 1854, he was made a partner in the Worcester, Massachusetts firm; however, four years later his interest in the firm was bought out by Warren William. The firm's name was changed to Ball & Williams and it ceased operations in 1865. Ballard stayed on with Ball & Williams as foreman until 1864.

Seven months after the outbreak of the Civil War, Charles H. Ballard was granted U.S. Patent #33,631 of November 5, 1861 which covered the Ballard action.

Ballard's improvement in breech-loading firearms *"consists in a novel construction of and mode of applying a movable breech for breech-loading; also, in the arrangement of all the parts of a lock of a breech-loading firearm within a slot in the movable breech; also, in certain novel means of bringing the lock to half-cock by the act of opening the breech; and further, in certain means whereby the cartridge-drawing device, after having drawn the cartridge, is returned to a recess within the barrel, out of the way of the movable breech and lock, by the force of the mainspring of the lock acting through the hammer."*[1]

A later patent was granted to Joseph Merwin and Edward P. Bray of New York City which allowed the Ballard to use a dual ignition system. In this case, the Ballard could use loose powder and ball with the percussion cap when rimfire cartridges were unavailable. Messrs. Merwin and Bray's U.S. Patent No. 41,166 of January 5, 1864 patent claim read:

"What we claim as our invention, and desire to secure by Letters Patent, is — The arrangement of the vent "g" and nipple "d" in the breech-piece B, in combination with the hammer D, the recess "e", nose "c", chamber C, and Shell E, as herein shown and described so that, without removal or alteration of the breech-piece, either fixed or loose ammunition may be employed, as set forth."[2]

The financial backing needed to manufacture the Ballard was supplied by the firm of Merwin & Bray. Their partnership had been formed in early 1861 with the expressed purpose of selling war materials to the government. Merwin & Bray had sales offices located at 246 Broadway, New York City; and in addition to having sole marketing rights for the Ballard, they were also the sales agents for Smith & Wesson, Pont, Plant, and Prescott revolvers.

The first advertisement placed for the Ballard rifle appeared in the March 29, 1862 issue of Harpers Weekly. This ad stated that the seven pound Ballard rifle was available in calibers .32, .38, .44 and came with a twenty-four inch barrel.

On June 2, 1862 Merwin & Bray requested the Ordnance Department to test fire a Ballard carbine. This test was performed by Captain Benet at West Point, New York. The Ballard carbine was fired one hundred times without the slightest fouling. It was fired at a rate of nine rounds per minute. Captain Benet concluded his report of June 13, 1862 by stating, *"Altogether it is the very best breech-loading carbine that has been presented to me for trial."*[3]

With Captain Benet's favorable report in hand, Merwin & Bray on September 8, 1862 offered to furnish the government five thousand

MERWIN & BRAY.

Breech-Loading Fire-Arm.

Nc 41.166.   Patented Jan. 5, 1864.

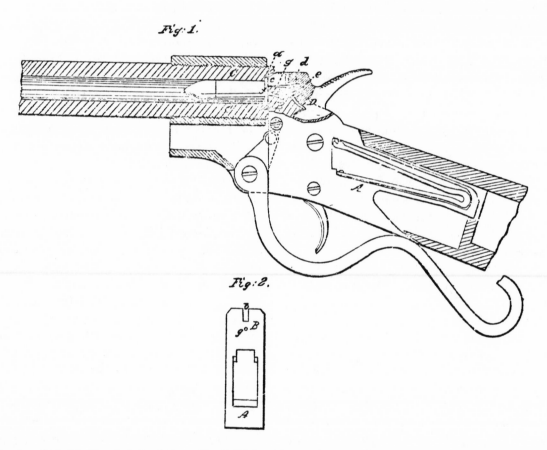

The drawing attached to Merwin & Bray's Patent No. 41,666 dated January 5, 1864 and quoted on the previous page. This ingenious modification allowed the Ballard to use loose powder and ball when the proper fixed cartridges were not available thus successfully addressing one of the most pressing concerns of conservative ordnance officers — the potential plight of units armed with breech loaders using special ammunition should they run out in the field and not be accessible to a source of supply.

Ballard rifles at $24.75 each and five thousand carbines at $23.00. Four days later the Ordnance Department gave an order to Merwin & Bray for one thousand rifles at $23.00, and one thousand carbines at $20.00 each with deliveries to be made in ninety days. A month later on October 14, this order was modified to reflect deliveries in six months instead of the previous ninety day timetable. The contract was finally signed by both parties on October 31, 1862.[4] This contract with extension would run for a year.[5] Merwin & Bray subcontracted for these arms with Dwight Chapin & Co. of Bridgeport, Connecticut.

The first of the .56 caliber Ballard rifles and carbines were completed by Dwight Chapin & Co. in March of 1863. On March 20, the sample carbine and rifle were sent forward to the Ordnance Department for their inspection. After being inspected, the Ordnance Department notified Merwin & Bray that both the carbine and rifle had been rejected because the breechblocks had not worked freely.

With the Ordnance Department rejecting these .56 caliber Ballard carbines and rifles, Merwin & Bray turned to the open market and sold six hundred of the .56 caliber rifles and all one thousand carbines to the State of Kentucky. The Ballard rifles were delivered on April 22, 1864 and the carbines five days later. The rifles were purchased at a price of $28.00 each while the carbines were sold for $26.00 each.

On November 16, 1863, the State of Kentucky and Merwin & Bray entered into a contract for one thousand Ballard carbines in .44 caliber at $26.00 each; one thousand Ballard rifles in .44 caliber at $27.00 each; and three thousand musketoons caliber .56 at $28.00 each.[6] The one thousand .44 caliber, half-stock, thirty-inch barrel Ballard rifles were delivered between January 28 and April 5, 1864. The .56 caliber musketoons (full stock, thirty-inch barrel Ballard rifles) were changed to .46 caliber by Merwin & Bray by letter of January 12, 1864 and confirmed by the Quartermaster General of the State of Kentucky on February 16. Deliveries of these three thousand musketoons now changed to .46 caliber were made between July 14, 1864 and March 17, 1865. All of the .44 and .46 caliber Ballard rifles on the November 16, 1863 contract were manufactured by Ball & Williams of Worcester, Massachusetts. Ball & Williams had taken over the manufacturing of the Ballards after Merwin & Bray had discontinued subcontracting with Dwight, Chapin & Co. due to their poor performance. This occurred in January of 1864.

While the State of Kentucky was purchasing 4,600 Ballard rifles for their state militia units, the Federal Government only obtained thirty-five Ballard rifles in .56 caliber with thirty inch barrels. These thirty-five Ballard Patent rifles were purchased by the Government on December 21, 1863 from James M. Latta (a civil provost marshall) of Fernandina, Florida at a cost of $36.00 each.[7] Payment in the amount of $1,260 was sent to Latta on February 1, 1864. These thirty-five rifles were delivered to Colonel James Montgomery, Commander of the 34th U.S. Colored Infantry. At this time period, Colonal Montgomery was in charge of a brigade consisting of his own 34th plus 3rd U.S.C.I. and 54th Mass. Inf. It appears that the thirty-five Ballard rifles were used by his men in their duties as sharpshooters.

In addition to these thirty-five rifles, the Ordnance Department purchased one thousand five hundred and nine Ballard carbines at a cost of $34,738.00.[8]

The Ballard rifles saw little service during the Civil War; however, large numbers of Ballard carbines were in the hands of the Kentucky troops. As of September 30, 1864, the 6th, llth, 12th, 13th, 16th Kentucky Cavalry plus the 4th, 30th, 37th, 45th, 52nd and 54th Kentucky Mounted Infantry were armed with three thousand four hundred ninety-two Ballard carbines.[9]

To interest other parties in purchasing the Ballard, this advertisement appeared in Harper's Weekly from February 11, 1865 to April 22, 1865. It stated in part: *". . . these rifles were used by Captains Crawford and Fisk on the Overland Expedition to the Pacific under orders of the U.S. Government. The general government and the State of Kentucky have about Twenty Thousand (20,000) now in active field service, of which the highest testimonials are received."*[10]

As previously stated, the Ballard Military rifles are found in .56, .46 and .44 caliber rimfire. The overall length of these rifles are forty-five and one-half inches and weigh eight pounds five ounces. The thirty-inch blued or browned barrel is held to the forestock by three solid, casehardened oval barrel bands. The barrel has a blade front sight and the rear sight is a single-leaf folding type with adjustable slide, graduated to five hundred yards. A sling swivel is found under the buttstock and on the center barrel band. On the rifles purchased by the State of Kentucky will be found marked "Kentucky" on the top facet of the octagonal section of the barrel. These markings are on the .44 caliber rifles and similar markings are on the .46 caliber rifles located on the top of the frame.

On November 16, 1863 the State of Kentucky entered into a contract with Merwin & Bray for 3,000 of these .46 caliber Ballard Rifles.
— Milwaukee Public Museum collection

The State of Kentucky also agreed, as part of their November 16, 1863 contract, to accept delivery of 1,000 of the .44 caliber, half-stock Ballard rifles with 30 inch barrels.
— Milwaukee Public Museum collection

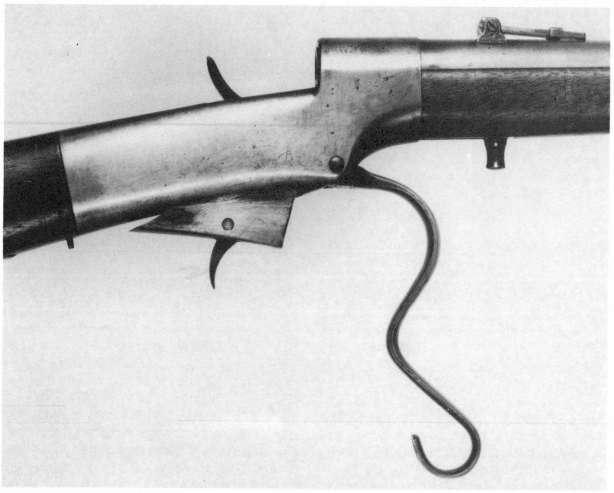

A close-up view of the action and rear sight of the Ballard rifle. Note the vertical knob cartridge extractor located forward of the receiver.

GOVERNMENT PROCUREMENT OF BALLARD RIFLES[13]

CONTRACTOR'S OR SELLER'S NAME	DATE OF PURCHASE	QUANTITY OR KIND OF STORES	PRICE	AMOUNT	DATE OF CONTRACT OR ORDER
James M. Latta	12/21/63	35 Ballard rifles	$36.00	$1,260.00	Open Market Purchase

The casehardened receiver is marked: BALLARD'S PATENT/NOV. 5, 1861 and BALL & WILLIAMS/WORCHESTER, MASS and sometimes MERWIN & BRAY AGTS./NEW YORK. The serial number is found on the barrel, receiver and hammer.

To operate the Ballard, the trigger guard is pushed down and forward which exposes the chamber for insertion of the rimfire cartridge. This motion of lowering the trigger guard brings the hammer to the half-cock position. After the rifle is fired, the spent cartridge is extracted manually by pushing the cartridge extractor which is the vertical knob found under the forestock. The knob is pressed back to extract the fired cartridge.

Shortly after the war, the State of Kentucky filed a claim with the United States Government for reimbursement for the amounts spent on the Ballard carbines and rifles. This claim was filed under the Indemnification Act of June 1861 which authorized recovery by the states for expenses incurred by them in defense of the United States. After the Treasury Department reimbursed the State of Kentucky for their cost, the Ballard carbines and rifles were sent to various federal arsenals for storage.

In December of 1868, the Springfield Arsenal sold sixteen of these Ballard rifles at $9.10 each and as late as September of 1876, six hundred sixty-two Ballard rifles were sold from the New York City Arsenal at $10.00 each.[11] The value of these surplus rifles had stayed fairly constant due to their great success as a sporting arm. The Ballard rifles would be commercially manufactured up until 1891 when production was finally discontinued. For the last fifteen years of their production, they were made by the Marlin Firearms Company of New Haven, Connecticut.

In the post war years, Charles H. Ballard moved to Newberryport, Massachusetts where a new factory was under construction to manufacture his rifles — now being manufactured by the Merrimack Arms and Manufacturing Co.

In 1869, he left Merrimack Arms and moved back to Worcester, Massachusetts where he started Ballard & Co. which manufactured a small single shot derringer designed by Lewis T. Fairbanks. With small demand for these derringers, the company ceased operations in 1872. Charles Ballard died in 1901.[12]

[1] U.S. Patent Office, U.S. Patent No. 33,631 of November 5, 1861.

[2] U.S. Patent Office, U.S. Patent No. 41,166 of January 5, 1864.

[3] National Archives Record Group 156-1001.

[4] National Archives Record Group 156-79.

[5] National Archives Record Group 156-81.

[6] Annual Report, the Quartmaster General to the Governor of the State of Kentucky for the Year 1863-4. Frankfort, 1865, p. 10-28.

[7] National Archives Record Group 156-164.

[8] John D. McAulay, *Carbines of the Civil War 1861-1865*, Union City, 1981, p. 94.

[9] National Archives Record Group 156-110.

[10] Harper's Weekly, February 11, 1865.

[11] National Archives Record Group 156-125.

[12] Edward A. Hull, *Ballard "Old Model" Firearms* (Part 1), The Gun Report, June 1985, p. 18-23.

[13] National Archives Record Group 156-164.

Tintype of a Federal Infantryman armed with a Colt Revolving Rifle equipped with a saber bayonet. Note that, like all Civil War photographs, the image is reversed accounting for the backwards hunting horn device affixed to his hat.   — Herb Peck Jr. collection

THE COLT M1855 REVOLVING RIFLE

By 1855 Samuel Colt was well established as a highly successful designer and entrepreneur. His revolvers had already been acclaimed as the best firearm for military service. While the credit for Colt's design was Sam Colt's, the way they were manufactured was the work of Elisha K. Root.

Elisha K. Root was born in Belchertown, Massachusetts on May 5, 1808. At the age of fifteen, he became an apprentice in a machine shop in Ware. In 1832, Root moved to Collinsville, Connecticut and went to work for the Collins Company. For the next seventeen years, he helped establish the Collins Company as the leader in the American axe industry.

In 1845, Root was offered the position of 'Master Armorer' at the United States Springfield Armory. He declined this offer and remained with the Collins Company until 1849 when he became superintendent of the newly formed Colt Armory at Hartford, Connecticut. For the next five years, Root designed and built the Colt factory as well as a majority of the machinery for it. He helped design machines for boring and rifling gun barrels, stockturning, splining and for making cartridges.

During this period, Root worked closely with Colt in the design for his various revolvers. On December 25, 1855, Root was granted U.S. Patent No. 13,999 for his exposed side hammer design. Root's design is the only percussion Colts which used the solid frame. The major designs characteristics of the Root are its cylinder enclosed by the frame, cylinder pin removable from back of cylinder and frame; side mounted percussion hammer which is bent to strike the center of the percussion nipple; and the creeping lever.

It is the so-called creeping lever design which was actually patented by E. K. Root on December 25, 1855. His improvement in revolving firearms consisted in combining the driving-pin that works in the grooves to rotate and hold the breech with a slide below having a loop or equivalent for the reception of the trigger-finger, by which it is moved back and forth, and adapted to act on the lock at the end of its back motion to operate the hammer and fire the load.[1] Root turned this patent over to his employer, Sam Colt.

While Root's patent was granted in December of 1855, no rifles were manufactured until 1857. During this period, additional time was needed to experiment to perfect the locking, unlocking and turning of the cylinder. The first government order for the Colt Root revolving rifles occured in October of 1856 and called for one hundred rifles at $50 each. On April 13, 1857, one hundred one of these rifles were delivered to the government. They were in .44 caliber, six shot per cylinder and with thirty-one and five sixteenths inch barrels. Between April 1857 and April 1859, a total of seven hundred sixty-five M1855 Colt rifles were obtained by the Ordnance Department plus sixty-four M1855 Colt Root carbines in 1859.

In 1859, the Navy tested the Colt at the Washington Navy Yards. Two .56 caliber rifles with thirty-one and three-sixteenths inch barrels were test fired by Lieutenant Lewis. In his report of July 22, 1859, Lewis stated to Charles Walsh, Acting Secretary of the Navy, that a .56 caliber Colt, Serial No. 209, was fired on July 18 and 19 a total of two hundred fifty shots at a target of five hundred yards with only seven misses. On the following two days, July 20 and 21, a Colt, Serial No. 424, was fired five hundred rounds at a distance of five hundred yards with thirty-eight misses. Lieutenant Lewis concludes his report by stating: *'During the trial of these pieces, the firing was deliberate. They were not cleaned, and sufficient time only allowed for them to cool when hot. They worked smoothly and easy. None failed to go off, and the cylinders showed less deposit than usual."*[2]

On September 9, 1859, the same date the Navy ordered nine hundred Sharps rifles and five hundred Joslyn rifles, they ordered from Samuel Colt one hundred M1855 Colt rifles. They were to be delivered at the Washington Navy Yards and cost the Navy $47.50 each. Deliveries were made on February 24, 1860. The total cost of this order amounted to $4,755.65.[3]

The M1855 Colt rifle also came in carbine and shotgun styles with various calibers ranging from .40 to .64 and barrel lengths from twenty-four inches to thirty-seven and one-half inches. The five shot military models 'Army Pattern' are in .56 caliber with a barrel length of thirty-one and five-sixteenths inches and weighing nine pounds fifteen ounces. The oil stained walnut forestock held to the barrel by two oval barrel bands of the clamping type similar to the ones used on the Colt Special Model 1861 Rifle Muskets. All metal is a dull blue except for the hammer and lever which are case hardened. The top strap of the frame is marked on the .56 caliber rifles with COL COLT HARTFORD CT USA. The fluted cylinder is without the roll engraved scenes. Between the flutes is stamped in one line PATENTED SEPT 10th, 1850. The ratchet-type loading lever used on these rifles was later used on the M1860 Colt Revolvers. The folding leaf rear sight is graduated from 100-300-500 yards with some to six hundred yards. The swelled end, button-head cleaning rod is located under the barrel with additional section of the rod carried in the buttstock. These .56 caliber rifles will take either the angular or saber bayonet.

The bullets used in the .56 caliber 'Army Pattern' were .58 inches in diameter, weighed four hundred ninety grains and were propelled by a powder charge of forty-five grains.

During the latter part of the 1850s, many of these Colt Revolving rifles were turned over by the Federal Government to be used by the various state militias.

For the fiscal year ending June 30, 1858, sixty of these Colt rifles had been transferred to

General Philip H. Sheridan — Famous Union Cavalry commander and the hero of Winchester. Sheridan commanded the 2nd Michigan Cavalry early in the War, a unit armed with Colt Revolving Rifles at the time he took charge on May 25, 1862.
— National Archives

the State of Connecticut. In the following fiscal year ending June 30, 1859, twenty more Colts had been sent to Connecticut plus one hundred twenty to North Carolina; fifty to Alabama; ten to Louisiana; one hundred to Virginia; and one to Ohio.[4] When the Confederates seized the U.S. arsenal at Baton Rouge, Louisiana in 1861, seventy-three Colt rifles were in storage at the arsenal along with a large quantity of flintlock and percussion muskets.[5] During the War, the lst Virginia, 3rd Texas and 13th Tennessee Confederate Cavalry were partially armed with the Colt revolving rifles as were the 8th Virginia and llth Mississippi Infantry.[6]

With the outbreak of the Civil War in April of 1861, Samuel Colt wrote to Connecticut Governor Buckingham on April 25 offering to raise a regiment of infantry to be known as the First Connecticut Regiment Colt Revolving Rifles. Samuel Colt would furnish his .56 caliber revolving rifles with twenty-seven inch barrels and weighing nine pounds and eleven ounces. Colt would furnish these rifles at $40.50 each plus sword bayonet. The next day, April 26, Governor Buckingham accepted Colt's offer. Enlistment in this regiment started on May 14 and two days later, Sam Colt was made Colonel of the regiment. After only a month of organization and regimental drills, the regiment was disbanded by the Governor by Special Order No. 307 of June 20. However, before the disbandment, Samuel Colt had delivered four hundred Colt Revolving rifles to the regiment.

This personal setback did not deter Sam Colt from giving his whole support to the Union cause. On July 5, 1861, he and General Ripley at the Ordnance Department entered into the first contract for the delivery of twenty five thousand rifle muskets at $20 each. The first deliveries were to be one thousand in six months. The Ordnance Department was to purchase one hundred thousand five Special Model 1861 Colt Rifle Muskets from Colt between September 26, 1862 and December 27, 1864.[7]

In the first year of the War, Samuel Colt furnished no M1855 Colt rifles to the Ordnance Department but did deliver, in 1861, fourteen thousand five hundred Model 1860 Colt .44 caliber revolvers plus five thousand twenty imported Enfield rifles.[8]

All purchases of M1855 Colt revolving rifles obtained by the government in 1861 were on the open market. On September 28, 1861 eight hundred sixty-one Colt rifles were purchased from Ben Kittredge & Co. of Cincinnati, Ohio for the price of $50 each, while another seventy Colt rifles came from C.J. Brockway on November 21, 1861.

While Samuel Colt furnished no revolving rifles to the government in 1861, Captain Harwood, Chief of Naval Ordnance, telegraphed Colt on May 24 asking if the Colt factory could furnish three thousand .75 caliber Navy muskets with thirty-four inch barrels and with saber bayonets. The following day Colt responded by stating that he could immediately deliver two hundred ninety of his .56 caliber revolving rifles with the triangular bayonet and within twenty days two hundred more, plus seventy-five per week thereafter.[9] Captain Harwood declined this offer and two months later, on July 15, entered into a contract for ten thousand .69 caliber Plymouth rifles from Eli Whitney.

Colt's first wartime contract for the M1855 Colt rifle was received by telegraph from the Ordnance Office on January 27, 1862. It stated:

"Send to Colonel Ramsay, Washington arsenal, one thousand Colt's repeating rifles and appendages, and one hundred thousand cartridges for the same."[10]

The price was set at $45 each with bayonet. Deliveries were made the following day — January 28 and payment issued on February 8.

Samuel Colt died on January 10, 1862, just days before this order was placed — Colts' place as President being taken by E.K. Root who would run the firm until his own death on July 5, 1865.

The Colt factory received three additional orders for the revolving rifles. These orders were placed between October 24, 1862 and January 25, 1863 for a total of two thousand seven hundred twenty-four rifles. On October 24, 1862 General Ripley wrote to E.K. Root:

"SIR: By direction of the Secretary of War, I have to request that you will immediately furnish this department with eight hundred and twenty-four (824) Colt's repeating rifles and appendages, of the same pattern as have been heretofore obtained from you, to be subject to inspection. The price to be $42 each, as mentioned in your dispatch to the Assistant Secretary of War of the 23rd instant, and to be paid for on the usual certificates of inspection and receipt by the inspector of contract arms."[11]

On November 17 General Ripley again addressed an order to Root — this time for nearly twice as many rifles:

"SIR: By direction of the Secretary of War, I have to request that you will immediately furnish this department with sixteen hundred (1,600) Colt's repeating rifles, and appendages, of the same pattern as have been heretofore obtained from you, to be subject to inspection. The price to be the same as paid for those purchased from you on the 24th October — namely, $42 each, and to be paid for on the usual certificate of inspection and receipt by the inspector of contract arms."[12]

Finally, on January 24, 1863 the final order was placed by the Ordnance Office:

"SIR: Please furnish this department, as soon as possible with 300 revolving rifles, calibre 56. How soon will they be ready for inspection?"[13]

During the Civil War, the Ordnance Depart-

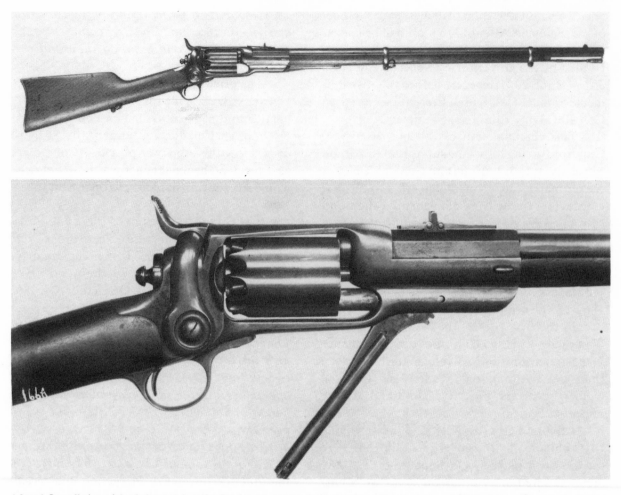

(above) **Overall view of the Colt revolving rifle. During the war the Ordnance Department purchased 4,613 of these rifles, most of which —3,725 — were obtained directly from the Colt Patent Firearms Manufacturing Company of Hartford, Connecticut. (below) Close-up view of the fluted cylinder section of the Colt-Root Model 1855 rifle.** Courtesy of the Smithsonian Institution collection.

ment purchased four thousand six hundred thirteen Colt revolving rifles of which three thousand seven hundred twenty-five were obtained directly from the Colt factory. In addition, Colt furnished the Government with two thousand fifty-six .36 caliber revolvers; one hundred twenty-four thousand one hundred fifty-seven M1860 .44 caliber revolvers; five thousand sixty imported Enfield rifles; one hundred thousand five rifle muskets plus ten thousand four hundred M1841 U.S. Rifles — all for a total cost to the government of $4,687,031.35.[14]

The best known of all the regiments to use the M1855 Colt rifles were Colonel Berdan's 1st and 2nd U.S. Sharpshooters. In the early campaigns around Richmond, Virginia in May of 1862, they used their Colt rifles with great effectiveness. During this period, the 1st USSS were armed with eight hundred eighty-six of these

five shot .56 caliber rifles.[15]

In the battle around Yorktown, Virginia in May of 1862, Berdan's Sharpshooters kept up such a deadly and continuous barrage of fire on the Confederate's artillery and trench positions that they were unable to man their artillery. The Sharpshooters of the 1st Regiment turned their Colts in on May 8, 1862 for the M1859 Sharps rifles while the 2nd USSS turned theirs in on June 1, 1862 at Fredericksburg, Virginia. However, before they did, they found the Colts to be overall a very acceptable rifle.

Two other regiments to have used the Colt rifles were the 2nd Michigan Cavalry and the 21st Ohio Infantry. The 2nd Michigan Cavalry was organized at Detroit, Michigan and mustered into U.S. service on October 2, 1861. The 2nd left the state for St. Louis, Missouri on November 14. As of May 1862, they were

GOVERNMENT PROCUREMENT OF COLT REVOLVING RIFLES[29]

CONTRACTOR'S OR SELLER'S NAME	DATE OF PURCHASE	QUANTITY OR KIND OF STORES	PRICE	AMOUNT	DATE OF CONTRACT OR ORDER
C.J. Brockway	11/21/61	70 Colt's revolving rifles with bayonets and appendages	$30.00	$2,100.00	Purchase
B. Kittredge & Co. Cincinnati, Ohio	9/28/61	123 Colt army rifles — Spring bayonets	$50.00	$6,150.00	Purchase
	9/28/61	48 Colt army rifles — Sabre bayonets	$50.00	$2,400.00	Purchase
	9/28/61	645 Colt army rifles — Spring bayonets	$50.00	$32,250.00	Purchase
	5/26/62	1 Colt revolving rifle	$40.00	$40.00	Purchase
Schuyler, Hartley & Graham New York City	4/23/63	1 Colt revolving rifle	$44.00	$44.00	Purchase
Colt Patent Firearms Co. Hartford, Connecticut	1/28/62	1,000 Colt repeating rifles with bayonets	$45.00	$45,000.00	1/27/62
	9/20/62	1 Colt rifle and bayonet, Caliber .56	$44.40	$44.40	Purchase
	10/28/62	824 Colt rifles and bayonets, Caliber .56	$42.00	$34,608.00	10/24/62
	11/22/62	1,600 Colt rifles and bayonets, Caliber .56	$42.00	$67,200.00	11/17/62
	2/16/63	300 Colt rifles and bayonets, Caliber .56	$42.00	$12,600.00	1/25/63

TOTAL   **4,613 Colt Revolving Rifles**   **$202.436.40**

assigned to the 2nd Brigade Cavalry Division of the Army of Mississippi.[16] On May 25, 1862, a little known Captain of the Regular Army, Philip H. Sheridan, was given his first wartime command when he was appointed Colonel of the 2nd Michigan Cavalry. At this time, the 2nd was armed with Colt revolving rifles, M1860 Colt revolvers and sabers.

In his first skirmish after taking over command, Colonel Sheridan's 2nd Michigan and the 2nd Iowa defeated a Confederate cavalry force near Booneville, Mississippi. In this skirmish of May 28, the 2nd Michigan fire power with their Colt revolving rifles was a determining factor in the defeat of the Confederate cavalry. With the defeat of the southern force, a portion of the Mobile and Ohio Railroad was destroyed along with the burning of twenty-six train cars containing ten thousand stands of small arms, three pieces of artillery, a quantity of clothing and the personal baggage of General Leonidas Polk.[17]

Phil Sheridan went on to become commander of Grant's Cavalry in 1864 while the 2nd Michigan would see continuous service until August 17, 1865 when they mustered out of federal service.

Like the 2nd Michigan Cavalry, the 21st Ohio Infantry was to serve the war armed with the Colt revolving rifles. The 21st Ohio had been organized at Findlay, Ohio and mustered into Federal service for three years on September 19, 1861.[18] As of September 30, 1863, ten days after the Battle of Chickamauga, the 21st Ohio was listed with two hundred forty-three Colt rifles.[19] In the previous battle, they with their five shot Colt rifles were able along with Wilder's Brigade to hold off repeated attacks from General Longstreet's Confederate Infantry. The 21st Ohio finally pulled back only after exhausting their ammunition of over forty three thousand rounds and being overrun by the Confederates. The remainder of the regiment would serve for the balance of the war and finally be mustered out on July 25, 1865.

The following is a list of Cavalry Regiments issued the M1855 Colt revolving rifle:[20]

    3rd U.S. Colored Cavalry
    4th U.S. Cavalry
    Ringgoldi Battalion
    1st Colorado
    2nd Colorado
    3rd Illinois
    7th Illinois
    9th Illinois
    15th Illinois
    2nd Indiana
    2nd Iowa
    7th Kansas
    1st Kentucky
    3rd Kentucky
    4th Kentucky
    7th Kentucky
    26th Kentucky Mounted Infantry
    2nd Michigan
    3rd Michigan
    4th Michigan
    1st Missouri
    3rd Missouri State Militia
    10th Missouri State Militia
    4th New York
    2nd Ohio
    13th Tennessee

Infantry regiments armed with the Colt revolving rifles included:[21]

    1st USSS
    2nd USSS
    7th U.S.
    8th U.S.
    9th U.S.
    10th U.S
    22nd Illinois
    27th Illinois
    37th Illinois
    42nd Illinois
    44th Illinois
    51st Illinois
    66th Illinois
    73rd Illinois
    74th Illinois
    98th Illinois
    12th Kentucky
    26th Kentucky
    34th Kentucky
    9th Ohio
    21st Ohio
    26th Ohio
    38th Ohio
    21st Michigan
    2nd Minnesota
    13th Missouri
    15th Missouri
    17th Missouri
    5th New Hampshire

As of December 31, 1863, seven hundred ninety-five Colt revolving rifles were in the hands of various infantry regiments. Those infantry regiments with forty or more Colt rifles were the 37th Illinois with one hundred fourteen; 12th Kentucky with fifty-seven; 26th Kentucky with one hundred nineteen; 34th Kentucky with one hundred six; 21st Michigan with fifty-five; 21st Ohio with one hundred seventy-four; and the 8th U.S. Infantry with forth-nine.[22]

The inventory records at the Forts and Garrisons as of December 31, 1862 show that they were armed with mainly second and third class muskets such as smooth bore muskets, Austrian and Prussian muskets. They had listed a few Sharps rifles plus seventeen .44 caliber M1855 Colt rifles in storage at Fort Leavenworth, Kansas and five .56 caliber rifles were at Fort Baker, College Mills, Kentucky.[23] During this same period, the various government arsenals and ordnance depots reflected one hundred twenty-seven unserviceable Colts in storage plus one hundred eighty-four serviceable Colts.[24]

The Ordnance Department during 1863-1864 polled the officers in the field to get their comments on the various breechloaders under their command. When polled on the Colt revolving rifles, twenty-nine officers returned their comments with eleven considering them the best arm in the service; five as very good; six good; five poor and two as worthless. The major complaints received were that the stock and locks broke most often; cylinder would not revolve and they get out of order easily. Captain A. E. Gordon's of Co. 'A' 2nd Michigan Cavalry comments were typical of those received in that "the arm is liable to get out of order and can't easily be repaired."[25] Even with these comments from the field, the Colt revolving rifles were to remain in Federal service throughout the war.

At the close of the war, the War Department issued General Orders No. 101 of May 30, 1865 and No. 114 of June 15, 1865 which allowed the soldiers to take their weapons home with them after having the value deducted from the muster out rolls. In this form, three hundred five Colt rifles were taken home at a cost to the soldier of $8.00 each.[26]

In the post war years, the Navy still listed forty-seven Colt revolving rifles of their original one hundred Colts in storage as late as December 1, 1866. Seventeen of these rifles were at the New York Navy Yard; twenty at the Philadelphia Navy Yard and ten Colt rifles at the Washington Navy Yard.[27]

The Ordnance Department, having no need for these obsolete rifles, sold them on the open market to the highest bidder. The following chart lists of some of the larger Colt rifle sales:

Following the war, along with all American arms makers, Colt suffered some setbacks. The company continued to grow however and remains today a leader in meeting our country's defense needs.

GOVERNMENT DISPOSAL OF COLT REVOLVING RIFLES[28]

DATE	NUMBER OF COLTS SOLD	PRICE PER ITEM	SALES FROM
January 18, 1866	409	$1.00	Alleghney Arsenal
November 25, 1867	72	$3.00	Levenworth Arsenal
April 1869	988	$2.00	St. Louis Arsenal
August 1871	736	4¾¢	St. Louis Arsenal
May 1882	900	.49¢	New York Arsenal
June 1882	71	.40¢	New York Arsenal
November 1882	38	.42¢	New York Arsenal
August 4 & 5, 1884	72	$2.00	Rock Island Arsenal

[1]U.S. Patent Office, U.S. Patent No. 13,999, December 25, 1855.
[2]NARG 74-145.
[3]NARG 74-157.
[4]NARG 156-118.
[5]Frederick P. Todd, *American Military Equipage 1851-1872 Volume II State Forces,* Chatham Square Press, 1983, p. 846.
[6]Ibid, p. 943, 1195, 1217.
[7]Ex. Doc. No. 99.
[8]Ibid.
[9]NARG 74-6.
[10]Ex. Doc. No. 99.
[11]Ibid.
[12]Ibid.
[13]Ibid.
[14]Ibid.
[15]R. Stephen Dorsey, *The Colt Revolving Shotgun,* The Gun Report, December 1975, p. 13.
[16]Frederick H. Dyer, *A Compendium of the War of the Rebellion,* Dayton, 1978, p. 1269 and 1270.
[17]Philip H. Sheridan, *Personal Memoirs of P. H. Sheridan,* New York, 1888, p. 149.
[18]Dyer, op. cit. p. 1506
[19]NARG 156-111.
[20]NARG 156-110.
[21]NARG 156-111.
[22]Ibid.
[23]NARG 156-100.
[24]NARG 156-101.
[25]NARG 156-215.
[26]Francis A. Lord, *They Fought for the Union,* Harrisburg, 1960, p. 166 and 277.
[27]House Exc. Doc. 16-2, 39th Cong. (Dec. 31, 1866).
[28]NARG 156-124 and 125.
[29]Exc. Doc. No. 99, 40th Cong., 2nd Session.

Target of 20 rounds made with Greene's breech loading Lancaster Rifle at 200 yards. Target 7 feet square — 2 shots missed the target. Small squares equal 1"

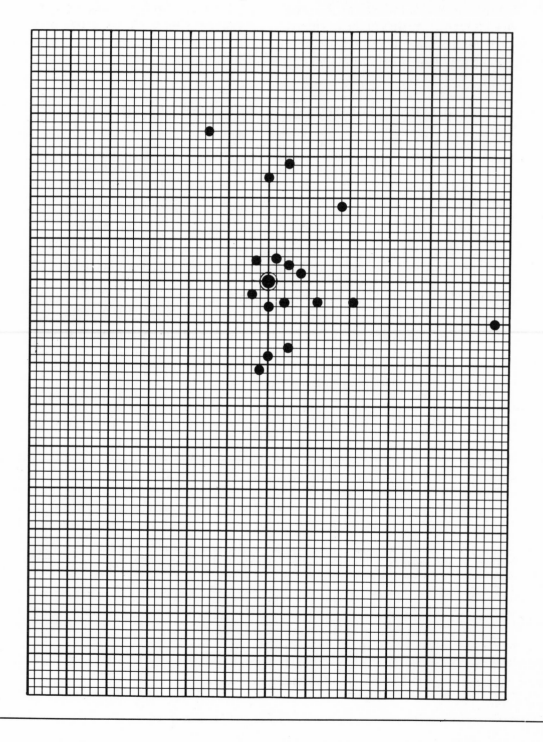

THE GREENE RIFLE

The Greene rifle has the distinction of being the first bolt action rifle purchased by the U.S. Ordnance Department. It was also the only rifle adopted by the government to have the feature of an under-hammer percussion system and oval bore rifling.

This unusual rifle was the invention of James Durell Greene of Cambridge, Massachusetts. He was born in Lynn, Massachusetts on May 12, 1828. His father, James Durell Green (1798-1882) was to serve as Mayor of Cambridge for a number of terms between 1846-1861. To distinguish himself from his father, Greene added the letter 'e' to his name,

Greene wished to attend West Point Military Academy, however, his mother objected to this since her brother had died while he was a cadet at the Military Academy. Greene would, therefore, enroll at Harvard and graduate in 1849 with a Bachelor of Arts degree and his masters degree in 1853.

In 1854 at the age of 26, he received U.S. Patent No. 11,157 dated June 27. This patent covered his .54 caliber breech-loading percussion carbine.

The manufacturer of the Greene carbines was Massachusetts Arms Co. of Chicopee Falls. In 1855, they entered into a contract with the British government for two thousand carbines. By 1857, all two thousand had been sent to England. During this time period 1855-57, the U. S. Government obtained three hundred Greene carbines of which one hundred seventy were used in the field trials of 1857.

In 1857, Greene first obtained a patent for the cartridge which was to be used in his bolt-action rifles. This patent was received on September 8, 1857 with U. S. Patent No. 18,143. This cartridge would have the bullet seated behind the powder charge and a felt wad behind the bullet. The patent describes the cartridge:

". . . consists in placing the ball behind the powder, and a wad of felt, leather, or other suitable elastic material behind the ball. The ball thus placed forces the wad against the joint between the breech piece and the barrel at the moment of discharge, and prevents the escape of gas at this point, while the elastic nature of the wad prevents the ball from upsetting, and enables it to be pushed forward with ease.

To enable others to understand my invention, I will proceed to describe the manner in which I have carried it out, and the construction and operation of my cartridge.

In the accompanying drawings are represented sections through the cartridge, in which 'a' is the ball; 'b' the powder in advance of the ball; 'c' a wad of felt, leather, or other elastic material which is secured behind the ball. This wad may be placed within the paper case, as in Fig. 1, or it may be secured to the outside of the case after the cartridge is made."[1]

This Greene bullet had a diameter of .546 inch and weighed five hundred forty-six grains. The combustible cartridge contained sixty-eight grains of powder and had an overall length of two and one-half inches.

Two months after securing his improved cartridge patent, Greene received U. S. Patent No. 18,634 on November 17, 1857 for his bolt-action rifle. This rifle had been designed to use his cartridge and had the following advantages resulting from the construction described above and may be recapitulated as follows: First, the ball, when forced forward by the breechplug, as in Fig. 5, is left with its axis coincident with that of the barrel; second, the force of the discharge causes the ball to compress the wad into the groove 'i' and over the joint, by which all leakage at the point is prevented.[2]

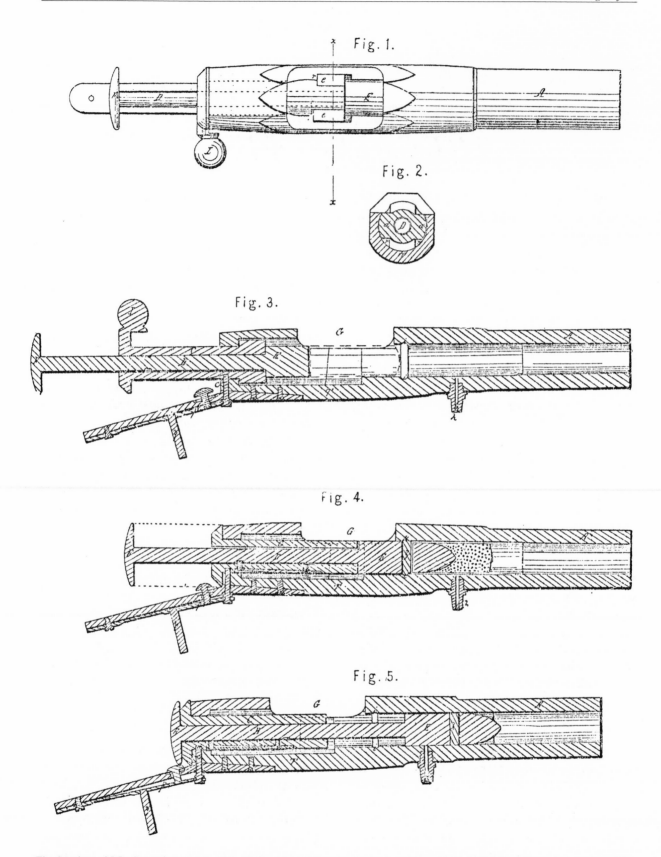

The drawings of J.D. Greene's breech loading rifle furnished with his first patent on the gun itself. A slightly earlier patent was issued to Greene for his special cartridge — about six weeks prior to the granting of this one, No. 18,634, on November 17, 1857.

Fig. 1.

Fig. 2

Actually issued about 9 days before the patent for the rifle it was designed to be fired in — these are the drawings attached to J.D. Greene's first patent — for his cartridge. Note that the bullet is at the rear of the paper cartridge. In order to fire the Greene rifle it was necessary to have two bullets in the chamber, one of which was at the rear and provided the gas seal.

Green's actual patent claim read:

"What I claim as my invention, and desire to secure by Letters Patent, is:

1. The groove 'i', or its equivalent, operating in connection with the wad at the rear of the cartridge, in the manner substantially as herein set forth.

2. I do not claim a sliding breech-plug secured to the barrel by ears and shoulders, as such device does not constitute my present invention; but what I do claim is the sliding breech-plug E, in combination with the revolving plunger C, operating in the manner substantially set forth.

3. The bolt 'c' and stop 'y', operating in the manner set forth, to interrupt the movement of the trigger, as described."[3]

Four years later Greene received U.S. Patent No. 34,422, dated February 18, 1862, for improvements to his rifle. This patent letter reads in part:

"My present invention relates to certain improvements on the breechloading gun for which Letters Patent of the United States were granted me on the 17th of November, 1857; and

it consists in attaching the hand-lever by which the sliding and revolving breech-plug is operated to the plunger which slides in the said breech-plug, so that the parts may be more conveniently manipulated."[4]

The operating of Greene's rifle was performed by:

"The parts being in the position shown in Fig. 1, with a bullet left from the last discharged cartridge in the rear end of the bore, (as represented by dotted lines at 'p') the button 'm' is depressed to unlock the plunger I, which is revolved by the hand-lever L a quarter turn, bringing the lever opposite the slot 'r' in the top of the barrel. The rod K is now pushed forward, as shown in Fig. 2, thrusting the ball 's' and wad 't' farther into the bore 'a'. The rod is now drawn back into the position represented in red in the same figure, with the hand-lever L against the cap J, when by a continuation of this movement, the plunger I is drawn back, as shown in Fig. 3. A cartridge is now introduced through the opening M, and is thrust forward into the bore 'a' by pushing forward the plunger I, the pressure being applied to the rear end of the cap J for this movement. Next, the plunger is again revolved by the hand lever L into the position shown in Fig. 1, when the stop 'n' locks it, and the piece is ready to be discharged, the powder of this cartridge lying over the nipple 'n', and its ball and wad against the breech-plug I, where the wad serves to pack the joint at the time of the discharge of the piece."[5]

His claim read:

"What I claim as my invention, and desire to secure by Letters Patent, is:

The combination of the sliding and revolving plunger or breech-plug I with the rod K, when the hand-lever L, by which the breech-plug is revolved, is attached to the rod, as set forth."[6]

It was a bolt action carbine which J. Durell Greene first had tested at the Washington Arsenal. This test occurred on August 2, 1857 with favorable results since three days later Colonel Craig at the Ordnance Department placed an order for one hundred bolt-action carbines for trial in the field. The price was set at $30 each including all necessary appendages. Interestingly, Greene refused to supply these since the

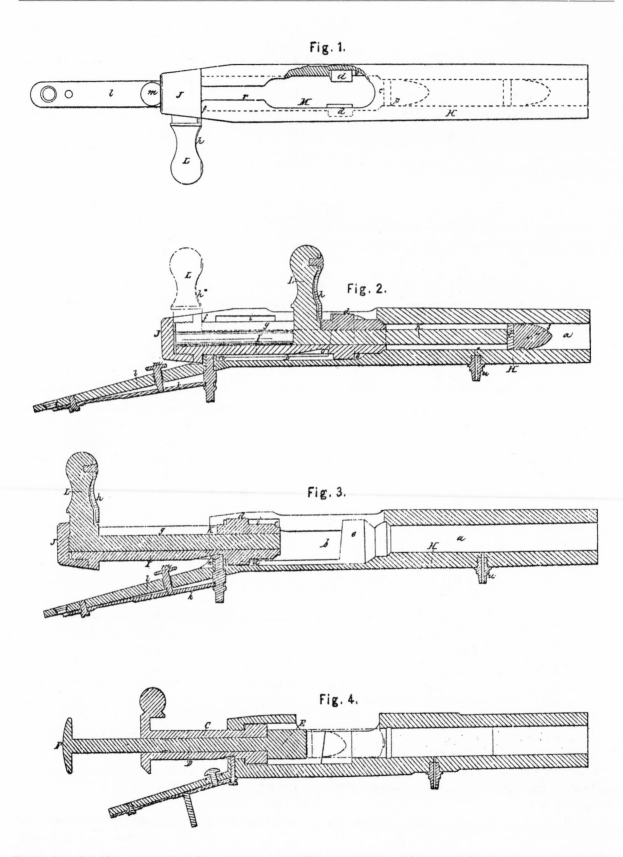

Fig. 1.

Fig. 2.

Fig. 3.

Fig. 4.

The drawings of his rifle attached to Greene's second patent — that of February 18, 1862 — which covered minor improvements in his largely perfected design.

cost of tooling-up could not be recovered from such a small order.

In 1859, Greene traveled to Russia and had his carbine tested. The Russians found the operation of the Greene very satisfactory and placed an order for three thousand infantry rifles. During this same period of time, the Government of Egypt placed an order for three hundred fifty Greene rifles. For their order the Russians advanced about one-third of their payment.[7]

In London Greene had purchased the oval bore rifling machinery from Charles Lancaster.

The Russian contract rifles were manufactured in the old armory buildings of A.H. Waters & Company of Millbury, Massachusetts. Between eighty and ninety skilled and experienced gunmakers were employed at the Waters Armory in the manufacturing of the Greene bolt action rifles for the Czar's army. This size of work force was able to turn out about three thousand finished rifles per year. The equipment was new and had cost Greene $18,000.

During the 1850's, J. Durell Greene had been in a number of Massachusetts militia units. He started as a captain in the Cambridge City Guard and before the war was the Colonel of the 4th Massachusetts Volunteer Militia. His commission as lieutenant colonel of the 5th Massachusetts was dated from June 23, 1860.[8]

With the firing on Fort Sumter and President Lincoln's call for volunteers, the 5th Massachusetts was formed at Boston on April 19, 1861. Two days later they left the state and were mustered into federal service at Washington, D.C. on May 1 for a three month enlistment.

While the 5th Massachusetts was camped near Alexandria, Virginia, Greene received a stallion fully equipped for service from Elias Howe, Jr., the inventor of the sewing machine. This event was fully reported in the *New York Express*.[9]

On Tuesday, June 25, 1861 at dress parade, Greene along with Major Keyes and Adjutant Barri took their leave from the 5th Massachusetts since all three had been promoted on May 14 to positions in the regular army. A letter was sent by the regiment to Senator Henry Wilson asking to have these officers retained with their command until the end of the regiment's three

month enlistment. Nothing came of this.

The May 14 promotion had made Greene the Lieutenant Colonel of the 17th U.S. Infantry which was being organized at Fort Preble, Portland, Maine. Greene assumed his duties with his new regiment on June 27. He remained with headquarters company of the 17th at Portland until June of 1863 when he took active field command of the regiment.[10]

With Greene in the U.S. Army, his father James Durell Green resigned as Mayor of Cambridge on July 24, 1861 to devote his full time to his son's gun business. It appears that a few hundred of the bolt-action Greene rifles were sold through the Boston firm of William Reed & Son. These arms appear to have been obtained by militia units, the exact identification of which is yet to be made. There has been no record of the Greene rifle having seen actual use during the war.

To interest the U.S. Government in purchasing the Greene rifle, J.D. Green wrote to Ripley at the Ordnance Department on December 21, 1861. Green offered to sell to the government the Greene at a cost of $35 each with deliveries of two hundred fifty per month.

Receiving no news from the Ordnance Department, Green arrived in Washington, D.C. on May 8, 1862 and went to see Secretary of War Stanton. He proposed to deliver five hundred Greene rifles now and a few thousand more in a year's time. The price was set at $32 each The same as Green was receiving from the Russian contract now nearly complete and ready for shipment. The number of Greene rifles actually shipped to Russia is unknown.

Two days later, on May 10, General Ripley directed Captain Thomas Rodman at the Watertown Arsenal, Watertown, Massachusetts to test the Greene rifle and report his findings back to the Ordnance Department.

On June 5, 1862, Captain Rodman wrote his report on his tests with the Greene. He was able to fire the rifle at a rate of nineteen rounds in seven minutes. Captain Rodman made the following objections against the Greene rifle as a military arm:

"1. The cone and hammer being on the underside of the piece, and very far forward, render the cocking inconvenient, the cap liable

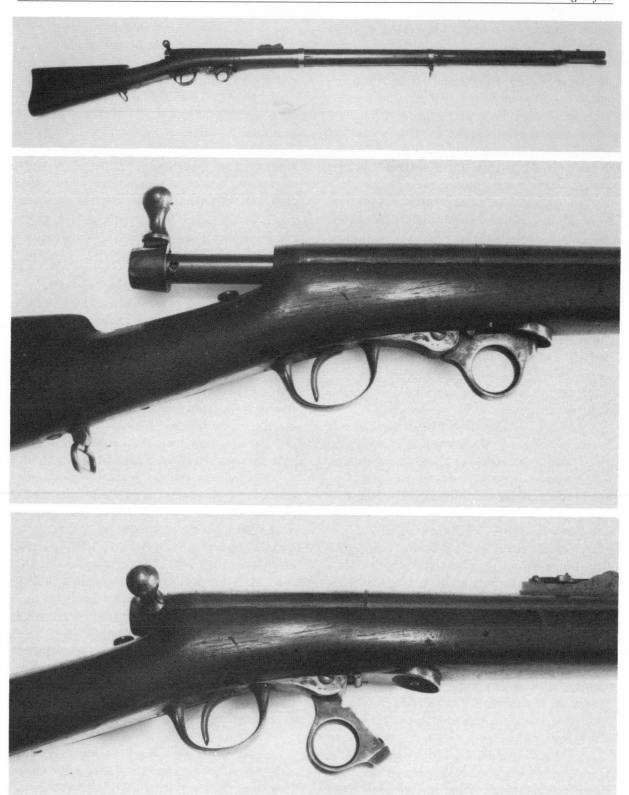

(above) The Greene was the first bolt action rifle purchased by the U.S. Ordnance Department — nine hundred of which were delivered to the Government on March 12, 1863. (below) Two close-ups of the action of the Greene rifle. Note the under-hammer percussion system the Green utilized. This rifle is serial No. 3157.

Authors collection

to fall from the cone, and the fingers and clothing of the soldier liable to be caught under the hammer in firing.

2. The cartridge, being inserted with the powder in front of the ball, renders it necessary to keep a spare bullet on hand, tear up, and throw away the powder of one cartridge, or fire a blank cartridge, before firing an effective shot.

3. The arm cannot be conveniently carried at a support.

4. It requires more motions, and more time, to load than a breech-loading arm should; facility in loading and rapidity in firing constituting the principal merit of breech-loading arms.

5. The escape of gas at the breech being prevented by the last bullet inserted, requires that every bullet with the cartridge paper around it should exactly fit the bore of the gun at the breech, a condition which could be very difficult, if not impossible, to fulfill in practice, where both arms and cartridges would be made at different places, and in large numbers.

In view of the foregoing I cannot recommend this as an arm for the military service."[11]

This did not stop Green because again on December 23, 1862 he wrote Secretary of War Stanton requesting an order for his rifle. This letter was forwarded to the Ordnance Department on January 3, 1863. Ten days later, General Ripley wrote to James Green stating that the government would place an order for nine hundred rifles with appendages. On March 12, 1863, the nine hundred rifles were delivered to the U.S. Ordnance Department. The price set was $36.96 each for a total cost to the government of $33,266.43. Cartridges were needed also and on March 30, 1863 Ripley wrote to James D. Green stating *"Cartridges for your rifles are immediately wanted. How soon can you furnish this department with 200 thousand? Reply by telegraph. Send a specimen cartridge to this office by mail with direction for making."*[13]

The Ordnance Department eventually secured one hundred seventy three thousand seven hundred sixty Greene cartridges at a cost of $3,869.82.

Green next turned his attention to the Navy Department. On August 29, 1863, Lieutenant Commander Eastman wrote his report on the test trials of the Greene. He stated that only twenty-eight rounds of ammunition had been supplied by the inventor for these test firings. The Greene rifle was fired at a distance of one hundred twenty yards. Of the twenty-five rounds fired, only one failed to hit the target.[14] Eastman's major concern with the Greene was he felt that the percussion cap being underneath would have a tendency to drop off the cone. He did not make any final conclusions on the Greene for possible naval use. There are no records of naval procurement for the Greene and it must therefore be assumed that no further action was taken by the Navy Department.

In early 1864, the Ordnance Department ordered further test trials on the Greene rifle. This test was conducted at the Washington Arsenal on March 8 by Captain Samuel S. Newbury. Cartridges used in this test were obtained from the owner, but the powder in the cartridges was found to be of poor quality. On the day of the test, the wind was very strong blowing from right to left which caused the wild flight of the bullet. The accuracy was found to be only adequate. The tests for accuracy were made at three hundred and five hundred yards. Thirty rounds were fired at three hundred yards and the last seven at five hundred yards. No hits were recorded at five hundred yards. Captain Newbury's report reads in part:

"37 shots were fired with care from a fixed rest. 5 struck the target from 3 different positions of the piece, but no position gave more than 2 hits in 10 shots."[15]

The report also states that the Greene rifle was satisfactory in regard to fouling, and that it cleaned itself well. The penetration of eight and one-third inches of boards was only fair.

Captain Newbury had been testing the Greene for possible cavalry use but concluded that the Greene rifle was altogether too heavy for mounted service and too clumsy. It would be difficult to load and operate the rifle while mounted. His opinion of the Greene was that it was a "decidedly inferior arm."[16]

Captain J.G. Benton forwarded Captain Newbury's report to the Ordnance Department agreeing that the Greene was not suited for cavalry because of its great weight. He ended his comments with:

"I do not know for what reason the 900 on hand here have not been issued. They, have not been asked for that I am aware of."[17]

These rifles remained in the Government Arsenals for thirty years after the war. On December 7, 1895, one hundred eighty Greene rifles were sold to James Moran for $2.50 each. By May of 1896, an additional three hundred thirty-two rifles had been sold to James Moran by the New York Arsenal.[18]

Turning to the bolt-action rifle covered by Green's patents, we find that its overall length was fifty-two and three-quarter inches and it weighed nine pounds fourteen ounces. This was over a half pound heavier than the Springfield rifle musket then in service. The stock is of oil finish black walnut. The thirty-five inch blued barrel has a blade front sight and long range rear sight graduated to eight hundred yards. While most of the Greene rifles were blued, some of the earlier ones will be found finished bright.

The three flat barrel bands are retained by conventional band springs. All other parts are blued except the case-hardened under-hammer and the bright steel ramrod.

The only markings found on the rifle are located on the breech tang reading:

GREENE'S PATENT/NOV. 17, 1857.
A serial number should be found on the underside of the bolt. Serial numbers have been recorded to slightly more than four thousand —tending to substantiate the theory that about four thousand Greene rifles were manufactured.

The oval rifling used in the Greene was the invention of an Englishman, Captain Birnes, in 1835. Oval rifling consists of a smooth surface, oval in cross section, revolving about the axis of the bore. A bullet which expanded to meet the inner surface of this bore was caused to revolve about its axis and had the advantage of cleaning out the powder residue with each firing.

The round .53 caliber bore was ovaled .008 of an inch on two sides to make the caliber .546 inch with one turn in fifty inches.

When we last left J. Durell Greene, he had just assumed command of his regiment in June of 1863. The 17th was attached to the Second Brigade, Second Division of the 5th Army Corps of the Army of the Potomac. The Second Brigade was made up of U.S. regular infantry

regiments consisting of the 2nd, 7th, 10th, 11th and 17th.

On the second day at Gettysburg, the Second Brigade was engaged against General Berksdale's Confederates in the Wheatfield. The seven companies of the 17th were to suffer one hundred fifty casualties out of about three hundred engaged in this battle.

Lt. Col. Greene's official report on the battle was filed on July 19, 1863 from Purcellville, Virginia. It stated:

"CAPTAIN: I have the honor to report that the Seventeenth U.S. Infantry, under my command, numbering 25 officers and 235 enlisted men, and forming a portion of the Second Brigade, Second Division, Fifth Army Corps, was engaged in the battle of Gettysburg, July 2.

The regiment formed the left of the brigade line, and went into action at 6 p.m. From the position in line, the nature of the ground passed over, and other circumstances, the regiment suffered severely from the fire of the enemy, as the list of casualties, recently forwarded, will show. The regiment was engaged in all about two hours, and retired with the brigade.

The regiment mourns as killed First Lieut. W.H. Chamberlin, and Second Lieut. E.S. Abbot, mortally wounded, young officers, but recently promoted from the ranks.

Both officers and men behaved with just credit under the trying circumstances in which they were placed. I particularly remarked Capt. E.H. Ludington, Company B, Second Battalion; First Lieut. A. Menzies, Adjutant First Battalion, and Second Lieut. F. E. Stimpson, acting battalion quartermaster, as distinguished for coolness and gallantry."[19]

In September Greene was given command of the 6th U.S. Infantry which was located at Fort Hamilton in New York Harbor and promoted to Colonel on September 20, 1863. Before he could settle into his new command, he received Special Order No. 571 of December 24, 1863 which detailed him as acting Provost Marshall General. Colonel Greene's offices were located at Madison, Wisconsin. His duties were to recruit troops for federal service. In a May 1864 letter written from Madison, Greene stated that the 36th and 37th Wisconsin Infantry were organized and ready for service.

GOVERNMENT PROCUREMENT OF GREENE RIFLES[22]

CONTRACTOR'S OR SELLER'S NAME	DATE OF PURCHASE	QUANTITY OR KIND OF STORES	PRICE	AMOUNT	DATE OF CONTRACT OR ORDER
James D. Green Cambridge, Massahcusetts	3/12/63	900 Greene rifles with bayonets	$36.96	$33,266.43	Purchase

As of June 21, 1864, Col. Greene having finished his recruiting detail returned to his regiment. Greene and the 6th U.S. infantry remained at New York City until May 21, 1865 when he was ordered to proceed with his command to Savannah, Georgia.

By General Order No. 71 dated August 31, 1866, J. Durell Greene was given the rank of Brevet Brigadier General U.S. Army for his gallant and meritorious service during the war. The brevet was to be dated from March 13, 1865.[20]

General Greene resigned from Army on June 25, 1867 and returned to Cambridge. He continued his study of firearms and received U.S. Patent No. 88,161 on March 23, 1869 and a later patent dated February 10, 1885.

After resigning from the army, Greene visited Europe and while in England, he was stricken with paralysis from which he never fully recovered. He never married.

At the time of his death on March 21, 1902, he was residing in Ypsilanti, Michigan. He was buried at the family lot, Mt. Auburn (Cambridge) Cemetary.[21]

[1]U.S. Patent Office, U.S. Patent No. 18,143 of September 8, 1857
[2]U.S. Patent Office, U.S. Patent No. 18,634 of November 17, 1857.
[3]Ibid.
[4]U.S. Patent Office, U.S. Patent No. 34,422 of February 18, 1862.
[5]Ibid.
[6]Ibid.
[7]Andrew F. Luskyik, The Breechloaders of James Durell Greene, The Gun Report, December 1971, p. 18.
[8]Alfred S. Roe, The 5th Regiment Massachusetts Volunteer Infantry, Boston, 1911, p. 320.
[9]Ibid, p. 56.
[10]Thomas W. Higginson, Massachusetts In the Army & Navy During The War of 1861-65, Boston, 1895, p. 181.
[11]NARG 156-1001.
[12]Ibid.
[13]NARG 156-7.
[14]NARG 74-145.
[15]NARG 156-201.
[16]Ibid.
[17]Ibid.
[18]NARG 156-124.
[19]Official Records, Part I, Vol. 27, p. 650 and 651.
[20]Thomas W. Higgen, Massachusetts In the Army & Navy During The War of 1861-65, Boston, 1895, p. 528.
[21]Alfred S. Roe, The 5th Regiment Massachusetts Volunteer Infantry, Boston, 1911, p. 321.
[22]Ex. Doc. No. 99, 40th Congress, 2nd Session

A paper carte-de-viste of a Federal Infantry private soldier, almost certainly taken very early in the war. In addition to the converted Hall rifle with its bayonet fixed note the arkward manner in which the subject wears his apparently new cartridge box and waist belt.

— Herb Peck Jr. collection

THE HALL RIFLE

The first mass produced breechloader ever adopted as the regulation arm of any country in the world was the Hall Breechloading Flintlock Rifle. This rifle also has the distinction of being the first small arm to be manufactured successfully on the basis of total interchangeability of parts.

The inventor, John H. Hall, was born at Portland, Maine on January 21, 1781. He was the first son of Stephen (1743-1795) and Mary Cotton (1754-1808). His father was a 1765 graduate of Harvard. He did not, however, take up his profession in Ministry but stayed on at Harvard as a tutor until 1777 when he moved to Portland and married Mary Cotton Holt.

Little is known of John H. Hall's early life. By 1808 he was engaged in the shipbuilding trade in Portland. In 1812, his shop was located near Richardson's Wharf and his residence on the corner of Fore and Cotton Street. With the United States at war with England, John Hall was part owner of a privateer — the sloop *"Yankee."* The sloop was to help prey on English shipping, but on her maiden voyage out of Portland, she was lost at sea and never heard from again.

During the War of 1812, John Hall was listed as a lieutenant in the Portland Light Infantry. Apparently he was later made a captain which title he would use for the remainder of his life.

Hall's patent for his breechloading system was issued to him and Dr. William Thornton of Washington, D.C. on May 21, 1811. This unnumbered patent is the oldest U.S. firearm patent in existence. This patent covered Hall's design of having a movable receiver raised at its forward end upward for loading at the breech instead of at the muzzle. Hall had the following discussion with Colonel Bomford at the Ord-

nance Department in regard to his patent. In a letter dated January 24, 1815, he states:

"I invented the improvements in 1811, being at that time but little acquainted with rifles, and being perfectly ignorant of any method whatever of loading guns at the breech."[1]

John H. Hall first applied to have his rifles tested by the government in 1813. With the United States at war with England, the government did not place an order for his rifle until January 1817 at which time they obtained one hundred rifles at a cost of $25 each. These rifles had been made by Hall in his Portland shop in 1816.

After successful testing Colonel Decius Wadsworth of the Ordnance Department entered into a contract with Hall on March 19, 1819. This contract called for payment to Hall of $1,000 for the right to manufacture at any of its public armories up to one thousand Hall breechloading rifles. Hall was to be employed at Harper's Ferry as assistant armorer and paid a salary of $60 per month. In addition, the government would provide Hall and his family free government housing plus pay a royalty of $1 for each Hall rifle manufactured at Harper's Ferry.

It took until 1824 to complete production of the first one thousand rifles. A second contract was signed in July of 1824 for an additional one thousand and finally a third contract on April 22, 1828 for six thousand more.

As previously stated in addition to being the first breechloaders, the Hall rifle was also the first to use interchangeability of parts. To produce rifles on this basis was an expensive task for the government armory at Harper's Ferry. By the year 1827, they had incurred a cost for machinery to manufacture interchangeable parts of $57,076.82. This initial cost was to show substantial dividends. The first lot of one thou-

3 Sheets—Sheet 1.

J. H. HALL.

Breech-Loading Fire-Arm.

Patented May 21. 1811.

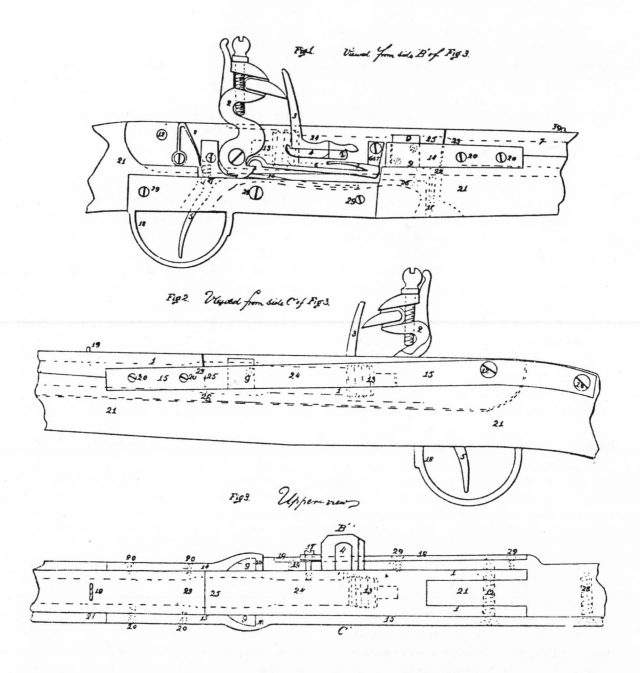

The first sheet of the official drawings registered with the Patent Office as part of John H. Hall's original 1811 patent. As mentioned in the text — this is the first U.S. patent dealing with firearms. Hall's apparent partner, Dr. William Thornton, was the Chief Clerk of the Patent Office and made an occupation of extorting half-interest in promising inventions in return for granting patents.

sand Hall rifles had cost the government $21.57 each to manufacture. However, by 1832 this manufacturing cost had been reduced to $14.50 each.[2]

The government wished to issue all Halls manufactured by Harper's Ferry to the regular army. By 1825, the Hall was in the hands of two companies of U.S. troops at Fortress Monroe, Virginia, In 1832, the entire 6th U.S. Infantry at Fort Leavenworth was armed with Hall rifles.

To supply the various state militias with a few Hall rifles, the government entered into a separate contract with Simeon North of Middletown, Connecticut. Simeon North had entered into his contract to furnish five thousand flintlock Hall rifles on December 15, 1828. The price for these rifles was set at $17.50 each. Between July 27, 1830 and July 25, 1836, five thousand seven hundred rifles were delivered by North to the Ordnance Department. The actual deliveries by year were six hundred rifles in 1830; eight hundred in 1831; one thousand three hundred forty in 1832; nine hundred in 1833; five hundred forty in 1834; eight hundred twenty in 1835; and seven hundred in 1836.[3] The North-Hall rifles are marked on the receiver US/NORTH/MIDLTN/CONN/over date such as 1832.

In addition to those supplied by North, Harper's Ferry manufactured twenty two thousand eight hundred seventy Hall rifles between late 1823 and 1844. The flintlock Model 1819 Hall numbered nineteen thousand six hundred eighty while three thousand one hundred ninety Model 1841 Percussion Halls were made. The last of the flintlock Halls were completed by September 30, 1840. By the fiscal year ending

September 30, 1841, one hundred ninety of the Percussion Model 1841 were completed and another three hundred were delivered by June 30, 1843. The final two thousand seven hundred of these percussion Halls had been completed by September 27, 1843. While the receivers on these Model 1841 Halls are found dated 1841 and 1842, it appears that they were completed first while the other component parts of the rifles were finished at a later date.

In 1840. John Hall took an extended furlough from Harper's Ferry and moved his family to Missouri. Two of his seven children went on to hold high political offices in Missouri. One son, Willard P. Hall, became Governor in 1864 and another a congressman.

In failing health, John Hall died at Huntsville, Missouri on February 26, 1841 before he could return to work at Harper's Ferry.[5] When the news of his death reached Harper's Ferry in March of 1841, the armory was closed for a day in his honor and a letter of sympathy was sent to Mrs. Hall.

Most of the Hall rifles manufactured were of the flintlock Model 1819. These rifles were .52 caliber and rifled with sixteen groves. The overall length was fifty-two and three-quarter inches and weighed ten pounds four ounces. The length of the black walnut stock is forty-nine and three-quarter inches.

The thirty-two and five-eighths inch lacquered brown barrel has a front sight and a dovetail 'V' notch rear sight. The uppermost one and one-half inches of the barrel is smoothbore at the muzzle to facilitate easier loading if it ever became necessary. The barrel is held by three barrel bands. Those rifles made between 1823 and 1831 will be held by the conventional band springs while rifles manufactured after 1831 have pin fastened bands.

The breech block, cock, frizzen, trigger, release plate and lever are all case-hardened. The trigger guard plate forms a very distinguished pistol grip to the rear of the trigger guard bow. The flat butt-plate is unmarked. The steel button-head ramrod is thirty-two inches long and threaded at the end.

The Halls are operated by pressing upward and rearward on the curved release lever located forward of the trigger guard. This allows the

---

PRODUCTION BY FISCAL YEAR OF HALL RIFLES AT HARPERS FERRY

1824	1,000	1837	1,200
1827	1,000	1838	2,934
1832	4,360	1840	1,023
1833	3,670	1841	190
1834	970	1843	300
1835	1,714	1844	2,700
1836	1,809		

Total Production 22,870[4]

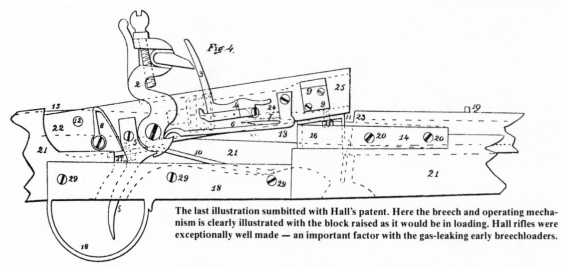

The last illustration sumbitted with Hall's patent. Here the breech and operating mechanism is clearly illustrated with the block raised as it would be in loading. Hall rifles were exceptionally well made — an important factor with the gas-leaking early breechloaders.

front of the breech-block to pivot upward to expose the chamber for loading of a paper cartridge or loose powder and ball. The powder charge consisted of one hundred grains of rifle powder and ten grains for priming the pan. The normal diameter of the bullet was .525 inches with a weight of about two hundred thirty grains.

The most common receiver markings are:

J.H. HALL	J.H. HALL
H. FERRY	H. FERRY
1824	U.S.
U.S.	1831

J.H. HALL	H. FERRY
U.S.	U.S.
1838	1841

The bayonet used with the Hall has a three inch socket, sixteen inch blade and an overall length of nineteen inches. These bayonets are similar to the M1816 musket bayonet.

The Hall underwent major changes when it went from flint to percussion with the Model 1841. With Captain Hall's death, in 1841, his name was dropped from the markings on the breech. Also, the M1841 lacks the pistol grip extension and the release lever was changed to what is now called the 'fishtail' type. The bore was rifled to the muzzle with seven lands and grooves instead of sixteen and the lower sling swivel was located to the rear of the guard plate.

By the outbreak of the Civil War, the Hall rifles had already seen previous service in the Black Hawk, Seminole and Mexican Wars. Commodore Perry took fifteen Hall rifles to Japan in 1854 — a gift from President Filmore to the Emperor of Japan.[6]

In April of 1860, the Federal Government sent one hundred twenty Hall rifles to the State of Virginia. They were in turn issued to the Virginia State Militia.[7] Between October of 1859 and October of 1861, the State of Virginia had issued one thousand two hundred twenty Hall rifles to the state militia infantry units.[8]

When the Confederate forces seized the U.S. Arsenal at Harper's Ferry in April of 1861, a number of Hall rifle barrels were utilized to manufacture a muzzleloading rifle. The gunsmith who undertook this task was J.B. Barrett of Wytheville, Virginia. The Hall barrel was plugged at the breech and provided with a nipple. A new stock was used as well as a new center-hung hammer which was pivoted in a brass frame fitted into the stock to the rear of the barrel. Only the barrel, barrel bands and trigger guard were used from the Hall while the remaining ensemble was entirely new. In addition, the Virginia Ordnance Department in 1862 altered and restocked about one thousand Hall rifles which were called 'Reed's Rifles'; however, they were found to be totally worthless arms.[9]

As the Confederates seized the various U.S. arsenals in the South during late 1860 and early 1861, large amounts of arms were turned over for Southern use. Among those arms captured were one hundred twenty-one Hall rifles from the State of Florida, seven hundred fourteen from Georgia, and two thousand two hundred

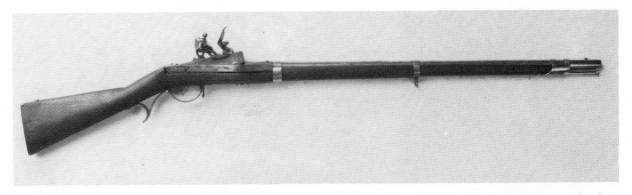

The Model 1819 Hall Flintlock Rifle in its original flintlock configuration shown here with the breech block raised as in the patent drawing opposite. Between 1823 and 1840 19,680 of these flintlock Halls were manufactured at Harpers Ferry and an additional 5,700 were turned out by Simeon North in Middletown, Connecticut.   — Smithsonian Institution

eighty-seven Hall rifles taken from the U.S. Arsenal at Baton Rouge, Louisiana. One thousand of these captured Halls were turned over by the Governor of Louisiana to the State of Mississippi. During 1861, five companies of the 24th Louisiana Infantry were armed with Hall rifles; however, by 1862, they had turned in their Halls for Enfield rifles.[10]

With the overwhelming demands placed on the U.S. Ordnance Department for arming the federal infantry at the start of the war, they purchased almost anything from the flintlock and smoothbore .69 caliber muskets to the more modern Enfield and Springfield rifle muskets.

With this vast shortage of small arms, the government went to the open market on August 7, 1861 and bought one thousand five hundred seventy-five Hall rifles from the Union Defense Committee of New York for $15 each.[11]

A few flintlock Hall rifles were still in use by the infantry in these early days of the war. One regiment partially armed with Hall rifles was the 2nd New Jersey Infantry. The 2nd had been organized at Camp Olden, Trenton, New Jersey on May 27, 1861. They left for Washington, D.C. on June 28 and were attached to the 2nd Brigade Runyon's Reserve Division of General McDowell's army.[12] When the 2nd left for Washington, they were armed with the .69 caliber smoothbore musket and one company with the M1819 flintlock Hall rifle.

At the first Battle of Manassas in July of 1861, the 2nd New Jersey armed with their smoothbore muskets and Hall rifles were held in reserve and did not take an active part in the battle. During the battle and afterward, they were assigned as provost guard to help round up the stragglers caused by the battle.

In 1862, the 2nd turned in their old obsolete smoothbore muskets and Halls and were issued the .58 caliber rifle musket. This regiment went on to see action in all the major campaigns in the East and was finally mustered out of federal service on July 11, 1865 at Hall's Hill, Virginia.

By December of 1862, all Hall rifles in field use had been turned in and replaced with more modern small arms. The fourth quarter summary reports of supplies in hands of infantry in federal service reflects that no regiments were still armed with the Hall.

The December 31, 1862 report of Ordnance stores at the different arsenals and Ordnance depots shows that two thousand four hundred nineteen Hall rifles were then in storage.[13]

HALL RIFLES
STORED IN UNITED STATES ARSENALS
REPORT OF ORDNANCE STORES
DECEMBER 31, 1862

LOCATION	FLINTLOCK	PERCUSSION
Frankford Arsenal	780	19
Springfield Arsenal	—	1
Washington Arsenal	—	1,551
Watertown Arsenal	—	21
Helena, Arkansas [Ordnance Depot]	45	—
West Point, NY [Ordnance Depot]	2	—
TOTALS	827	1,592

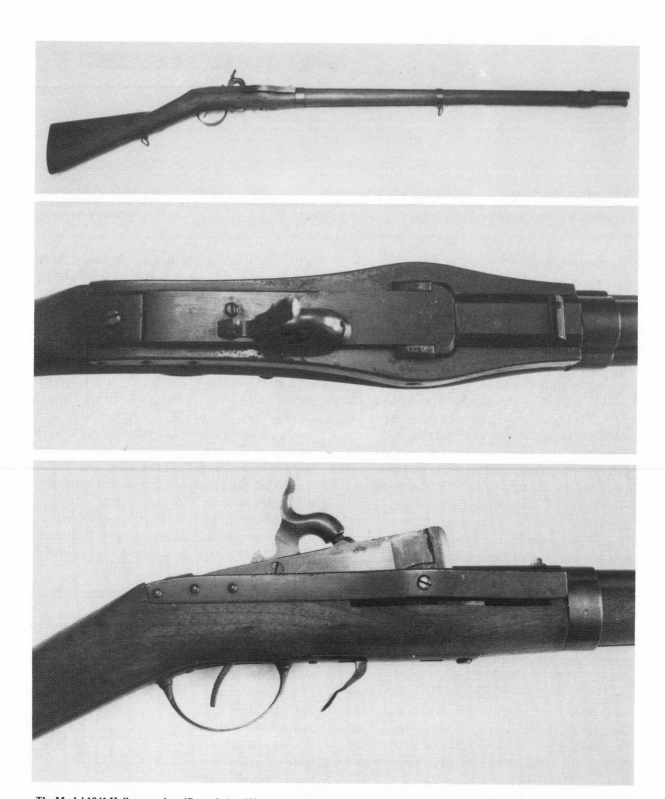

The Model 1841 Hall percussion rifle — the last if its type. Manufactured at Harpers Ferry, only 3,190 of these late Halls were made. The trigger guard no longer has the pistol grip extension and there is a new type of locking lever. The rear sling swivel is now mounted on the butt stock to the rear of the trigger guard rather than on the front of the trigger guard bow as with the Model 1819 rifle. Note the rear sight notch. All Hall rifles had the cock or hammer offset to the right and the sights offset to the left. It is virtually impossible to aim and fire one of them from a left-handed position.

— Author's collection

GOVERNMENT PROCUREMENT OF HALL RIFLES[15]

CONTRACTOR'S OR SELLER'S NAME	DATE OF PURCHASE	QUANTITY OR KIND OF STORES	PRICE	AMOUNT	DATE OF CONTRACT OR ORDER
Union Defense Committee of New York	8/7/61	1,575 Hall's rifles	$15.00	$23,625.00	Purchase

The Hall had come to the close of its colorful history in federal service and was to remain in storage for the balance of the war.

After the war, with the government trying to unload its vast supplies of small arms, one hundred fifty-eight Hall rifles were sold in 1868 at prices ranging from 14½ cents to 75 cents each. In June of 1869, William Read & Sons of Boston purchased one thousand twenty flintlock Hall rifles at $2.25 each. In August of the same year, they purchased an additional eighty flintlock Halls and finally in May of 1870, another one thousand at $2.25 each. All of the Hall rifles obtained by William Read & Sons were purchased from the government ordnance sales agency in New York City. As late as October 1, 1896, sixty percussion Hall rifles were sold at a price of $1.50 each.[14]

Because it was long obsolete when the Civil War began, the Hall breechloader saw relatively little field use. Nevertheless, it did see some and that in the early days of the war when functioning small arms were at a premium and anything that would work was desperately needed on both sides. Often not very well liked by the troops it was issued to, the Hall remained in service for a remarkable forty-five years — a fitting tribute to the first breechloader adopted by the United States and the yankee inventor who created it.

Charlotte J. Fairbairn and C. Meade Patterson, *Captain Hall, Inventor,* The Gun Report, October 1959, p. 8.
[2]Claude E. Fuller, *The Breech-Loader in the Service 1816-1917,*New Milford: 1965, p.27.
[3]R.T. Huntington, *Hall's breechloaders,* York: 1972, p. 233.
[4]Fuller, op. cit. p. 40.
[5]Fairbairn and Patterson, op. cit. p. 21
[6]S.E. Brown, Jr., *The Guns of Harper's Ferry,* Berrysville: 1968, p. 72.
[7]NARG 156-118.
[8]Frederick P. Todd, *American Military Equipage 1851-1872 Volume II State Forces,* Chatham Squire Press, Inc., 1983, p. 1266
[9]Ibid, p. 1207.
[10]Ibid, p. 717, 735, 846 and 851.
[11]Ex. Doc. No. 99, 40th Congress, 2nd Session.
[12]Frederick H. Dyer, *A Compendium of the War of Rebellion,* Vol. 2, Dayton: 1978, p. 1356.
[13]NARG 156-101.
[14]NARG 156-124.
[15]Ex. Doc. No. 99, 40th Congress, 2nd Session.

An unknown Union cavalryman armed with a Henry rifle. Note that the rear sight is mounted on the breech. — Herb Peck Jr. collection.

THE HENRY RIFLE

The most advanced repeating rifle to see service during the Civil War was the Henry. This rifle, with its fifteen cartridge magazine, raised havoc on the Confederate forces during the last two years of the war. It was often overheard said by the Confederates, "Give us anything but your d--d Yankee rifle that can be loaded Sunday and fired all the week."[1]

The origin of the Henry rifle occurred a decade before the outbreak of the war. In August of 1849, Walter Hunt received a patent for a magazine gun. Hunt lacking capital for his rifle assigned over his patent rights to George A. Arrowsmith of New York City. The task of making improvements to Hunt's design fell on Lewis Jennings. With these additional improvements being made, Jennings took out his own patent on December 25, 1849 with U.S. Patent No. 6,973. The Jennings' magazine rifle used hollow loaded bullets carried in a tubular magazine below the barrel, fed to the barrel by the action of a ratchet operated by a ring trigger. The Jennings' rifles were fired by a Maynard-type primer held in a priming magazine on the top of the frame. These rifles were manufactured by Robbins and Lawrence of Windsor, Vermont starting in 1850.

During this same period, Horace Smith was developing a magazine gun. His patent was issued on August 26, 1851 with U.S. Patent No. 8317. In 1852, Smith while working for Allen, Brown and Luther, manufacturers of rifle barrels, met Daniel B. Wesson which would form the famed firm of Smith and Wesson. These two men along with B. Tyler Henry's help made further improvements to both the Jennings and Smith patents which lead to a further U.S. Patent of February 14, 1854 with No. 10,535. This Smith and Wesson patent covered the trigger guard design which would be a forerunner on all later Henry and Winchester lever-action firearms.

In 1855, Smith and Wesson secured Rollin White's patent on a revolver with a chamber bored clear through. They decided to devote their full attention to the manufacturing of revolvers and, therefore, sold the rights for their repeating arms to the newly formed Volcanic Repeating Arms Company. In exchange for the machinery and inventory on hand, Smith and Wesson received $64,000 cash plus 2,800 shares of stock. In August of 1855, the Volcanic Company removed the Smith and Wesson inventory from Norwich and relocated at New Haven, Connecticut. The Volcanic Repeating Arms Company was short lived for on February 3, 1856 they voted to go into bankruptcy and assign over their property to their creditors with final insolvency declared in February of 1857. Oliver F. Winchester, the major stockholder in the Volcanic Repeating Arms Company, was by court order of March 15, 1857 given title to the entire assets of the Volcanic Company. He reorganized the company as the New Haven Arms Company on April 3, 1857. The New Haven Arms Company continued the production of the Volcanic line of repeating lever action pistols and carbines. During the period 1857-1860, about 3,200 Volcanic's were manufactured.

The master machinist on the development of these magazine arms was Benjamin Tyler Henry (1821-1898). B. Tyler Henry was born on March 22, 1821 at Claremont, New Hampshire. He first worked as an apprentice with J.B. and R.B. Ripley, gunsmiths, of Claremont and later at the U.S. Springfield Armory. In 1842 he left Springfield and went to work for Nicanor Kendall. Kendall would go into partnership with Robbins and Lawrence. It was at the Robbins and Lawrence factory that Henry worked on improvements to the Jennings magazine gun design in 1850. In 1854 when Smith and Wesson took up production of their lever-action firearms, Henry was hired as superintendent. He left Smith and Wesson and went with first the Volcanic Repeating Arms Company and later with the New Haven Arms Company as superintendent. At the New Haven Arms Company, Henry first went to work making minor refinements to the Volcanic pistols and carbines. He first substituted brass instead of a cast iron receiver, blued the barrels plus the barrels were left full octagon.

In 1860, the New Haven Arms Company abandoned the manufacturing of Volcanic rifles and pistols using loaded bullets and went to work upon the Henry rifles which used rimfire copper cartridges. The .44 caliber rimfire ammunition manufactured at the New Haven Arms Company were stamped on the head of the cartridge "H" (for Henry). The cartridge became known as the Henry .44 Flat. This cartridge held twenty-five grains of black powder, giving its two hundred sixteen grain bullet a muzzle velocity of 1125 f.p.s. The overall length of the case was eighty-five hundredths inch.

The Henry rifle which used this .44 Henry Flat cartridge was patented by B. Tyler Henry on October 16, 1860 with U.S. Patent No. 30,446.

"My invention relates to improvements in a repeating breech-loading gun designed and arranged for the exclusive use of a hollow loaded ball with a primer inserted in the base.

My improvements are designed to remove the objections heretofore existing in this class of fire-arms by a change in the construction of the moving parts and the addition of new features, adapting the arm to the use of a solid ball enclosed in a metal cartridge, this greatly increasing the power and certainty of fire of the arm."[2]

"What I claim therein is:

1. In combination with the hollow breech-pin N and the piston I, working through and with it, the giving of said piston additional end motion for the purpose of exploding the fulminate, substantially as described.

2. In combination with the hollow breech-pin and the piston working through it, the springcatch and rest on the breech-pin, and the fillets on the piston, substantially as and for the

purpose set forth.

3. In combination with the carrier-block C and the spring S, placed on top of the breech-pin J, the so forming of the top of said carrier-block near the rear end, as shown at 'z z', and thus raising the forward end of the cartridge while the rear end is held down by the spring-catch, tripping it over and freeing it from the spring and ejecting it from gun, substantially as described."[3]

The rights to Henry's October 16 patent were assigned to his employer, Oliver F. Winchester.

The Henry rifle is loaded by pressing the magazine spring all the way forward into the muzzle section, turning this section on its axis to expose the magazine for inserting of the fifteen rimfire cartridges. The muzzle section is then returned to its closed position which enables the spring to exert pressure on the row of cartridges. The lowering of the operating lever forced the block rearward which cocked the hammer in the same motion. This motion also fed the lower cartridge automatically into the breech and with the returning of the operating lever to its closed position drives the cartridge into the chamber.

With the outbreak of the war, Oliver Winchester traveled to Washington to visit the Ordnance Department. He called on Colonel Ripley and after exhibiting and explaining the Henry rifle to him, Ripley stated, "I believe that nine-tenths of the army officers will agree with me that they would prefer the old flint lock musket to any of the improved firearms."[4] Seeing that the Ordnance Department would not call for test trials for the Henry, Winchester, on June 18, 1861, wrote to Secretary of War Simon Cameron, "We desire to call the attention of the Federal Government to a new Repeating Breech-loading rifle now being manufactured by us, which is acknowledged by many competent judges to possess great advantages over any other rifle, and to be free from most, if not all the objections to the breech-loading arms now in use. . . Our object is to request you to appoint some competent officer who may now be in this vicinity to give the matter a preliminary examination, and if he reports in favor of the Government examining the subject further, then that a board of officers be appointed to give the arm a thorough

Color Bearers and Guard, 7th Illinois Volunteer Infantry. Photo by Mathew B. Brady. — Illinois State Library.

test at West Point, or some other suitable place."[5] Winchester's letter continues by stating that in September the production of Henry rfles would be two hundred per month and if necessary they could double that number.

In the following months the Henry would be tested by various officers. On November 19, 1861, Captain G. D. DeRussy of the 4th Artillery test fired a Henry repeating rifle at the direction of Colonel H.J. Hunt. Captain DeRussy reported, "In my opinion a most useful addition to the weapons we now have in service."[6] Three days before on November 16, Colonel Kingsbury, Chief of Ordnance for the Army of the Potomac, had written the Ordnance Department, "I think it would be well to purchase a number sufficient for one regiment ... With the barrel lengthened, it would be an efficient Arm

for Skirmishers, and with Carbine Attachment for Cavalry, Henry rifle appears to be quite equal to any in service, in the compactness of its machinery and the accuracy of its fire, and superior to others in that it may be fired fifteen times without reloading, and would not ordinary require to be loaded at all in the saddle."[7]

Brigadier General James Ripley would again put a damper on the Federal Government purchasing the Henry rifle when on December 9, 1861 he wrote Secretary of War Cameron stating his objections to the Henry. He regarded the weight of the arm with the loaded magazine as objectionable and the need for special ammunition rendering the rifle impossible to use with ordinary cartridges or with powder and ball. In addition, Ripley saw no advantages in rate of five over several of the other breechloaders already in service use. He concluded his letter to Cameron by advising that neither the Henry or Spencer rifle be purchased by the Government.

Once again General Ripley had curtailed the purchase of the Henry Repeating rifle. However, the testimony in favor of the Henry continue to come forth, this time with a report of Lieutenant W. Mitchell U.S.N. written on May 20, 1862 to J.A. Dahlgren, Commander of Ordnance at the Washington Navy Yard. Lieutenant Mitchell's report states in part:

"The rifle was fired on the 16th and 17th inst. as follows: For time or rapidity, 187 shots were fired in 3 minutes 36 seconds. These were fired in rounds of 15 shots each, the actual time of firing only counted. One round (15 shots) were fired in 10.8 seconds; 120 shots were loaded and fired in five minutes and forty-five seconds. This includes the whole time from the first shot to the last.

One target was placed at a distance of 328 feet, and the other at 728 feet. 120 shots were fired at 328 feet; 270 shots were fired at target at 728 feet.

It is due to the inventor to say that these shots are not a fair test of accuracy, as many of them were fired by a person unaccustomed to rifle shooting. Fifteen shots were fired for accuracy at a target 18 inches square, at 348 feet distance. Fourteen hit direct.

The firing was then continued to test endurance, &c., up to 1,040 shots, the gun not having been cleaned or repaired from the first shot. The piece was then carefully examined, and found considerably leaded and very foul, the lands and grooves not being visible. In other respects it was found in perfect order.

It is manifest from the above experiment that this gun may be fired with gread rapidity, and is not liable to get out of order.

The penetration, in proportion to the charge used, compares favorable with that of other arms."[8]

While Winchester's letter of June 18, 1861 to Cameron stated that by September of 1861 the factory would be producing two hundred Henry rifles per month, this timetable was not met. It was not until 1862 that the production of the Henry commenced in force. In that year about one thousand five hundred rifles were

Brigadier General James W. Ripley, Chief of Ordnance, was not in favor of repeating firearms at the outbreak of the war.
— National Archives.

turned out at the New Haven Arms Company factory. These first Henrys were sold on the open market with many being purchased by Kentucky troops. In a letter to Oliver Winchester of March 3, 1863, he was notified that fifteen men of the 12th Kentucky cavalry while on patrol were attacked by two hundred forty Confederate cavalry in an open lane and successfully repulsed and drive them from the field by the fire power of the Henry rifles.

In a July 1863 skirmish with Confederate General John Hunt Morgan's cavalry, Captain James Wilson of Co. "M" 12th Kentucky Cavalry reported that his men with Henry rifles were attacked by three hundred seventy five of Morgan's men. "I had only 67 men. The fight lasted about two and a half hours, we drove them about one mile, and that was the last we saw of them. We killed thirty one and wounded forty three. I myself lost six killed and wounded. I that night crossed the river with my company."[9]

The Ordnance Department finally on June 16, 1863 and four days later ordered a total of two hundred forty Henry rifles at a cost of $36 each. These orders were placed by Brigadier

Benjamin Tyler Henry (1821-1898). A master machinist and inventor, received patent number 30,446 for his "Magazine Firearm" design on October 16, 1860.
— Courtesy, Buffalo Bill Historical Center

General Ripley, the same man whom less than two years before was totally against the Henry. Ripley's letter to Oliver Winchester of June 20th, 1863, stated:

"SIR: Please furnish immediately one hundred and twenty (120) Henry repeating rifles at thirty-six dollars ($36) each; also two hundred cartridges for each rifle. Send them by quick conveyance to Colonel Ramsay, United States arsenal, Washington, D.C., and report their shipment by telegraph."[10]

A month later on July 23, two hundred forty one Henry rifles were delivered to the Ordnance Department and payment was made on July 25.[11] The largest order for the Henry occurred on the last day of 1863 when the new Chief of Ordnance, General George Ramsay, placed an order for eight hundred rifles.

"SIR: Be pleased to furnish for the use of this department eight hundred (800) Henry's repeating rifles. They will be inspected at the armory where made by Lieutenant Colonel Thornton, inspector of small arms. You will be paid at the rate of Thirty-six dollars ($36) for each rifle, including all the appendages neces-

sary for their use in service, upon the usual certificates of inspection and receipt, in such funds as the Treasury Department may provide. They are to be packed in boxes of a good and approved pattern, with as many in each box as the inspector shall direct, for which a fair price to be determined by him will be paid. Be pleased to signify at once your acceptance or non-acceptance of the above."[12]

The Henry rifles purchased by the Ordnance Department in 1863 are found in serial range from 3,000 to 4,200. The barrel and frame are marked with the initials C.G.C. for Charles G. Chandler.

The following government order for Henry rifles was not placed until the final days of the war when, on April 7, 1865, five hundred were ordered.

"SIR: You will please furnish this department, and deliver to the inspector of contract arms, five hundred (500) Henry's repeating rifles, for which you will be paid at the rate of Thirty-eight dollars ($38) for each rifle that may be received by the United States inspector. These rifles are to be furnished with all the appendages necessary for their use in service, and are to be delivered as early as possible."[13]

The final order was placed on May 16th for one hundred twenty-seven rifles.

"SIR: You will please furnish this department, and deliver to the inspector of contract arms, one hundred and twenty-seven (127) Henry's repeating rifles and appendages, for which you will be paid at the rate of thirty-eight ($38) each for all that pass the usual inspection."[14]

In addition to the one thousand seven hundred thirty Henry rifles purchased from the New Haven Arms Company at a cost of $63,546 the Government also purchased from them one Henry carbine on November 7, 1865 for $35. Four million six hundred ten thousand four hundred (4,610,400) Henry cartridges were purchased by the Ordnance Department at a cost of $107,353.05.

The earliest of the Henry rifles are found with iron frames while the majority have frames made of brass. These early iron frame Henry's are also found without a catch for the operating lever which is found on the brass frame model.

The Henry rifles have an overall length of

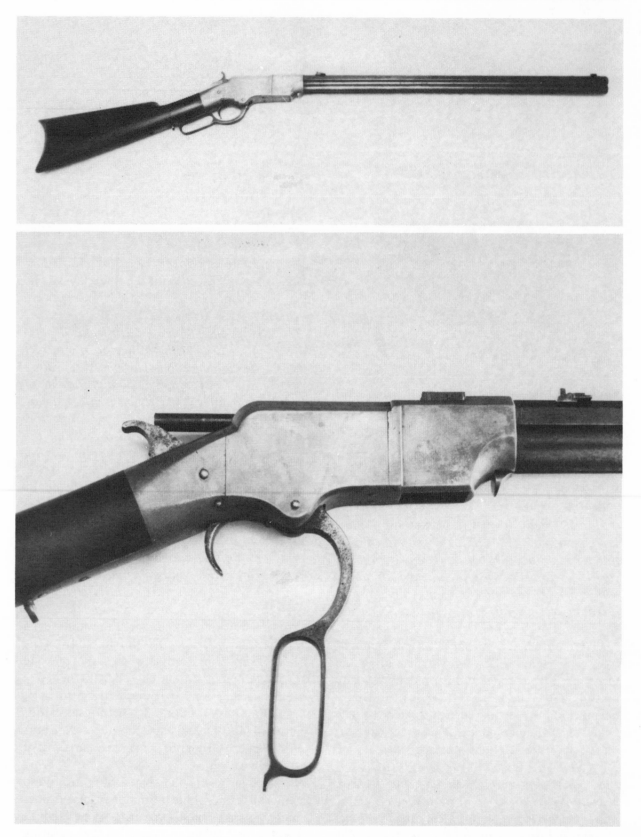

Overall view and close-up of the breech section of the Henry rifle. Lowering the operating lever forces the block to the rear which, in turn, cocks the hammer. Returning the lever to the closed position feeds the .44 caliber Henry rimfire cartridge into the chamber. In total about 13,500 Henry rifles were manufactured between 1860 and 1866. The rifle illustrated here is serial number 5310. — Authors collection

GOVERNMENT PROCUREMENT OF HENRY RIFLES[23]

CONTRACTOR'S OR SELLER'S NAME	DATE OF PURCHASE	QUANTITY OR KIND OF STORES	PRICE	AMOUNT	DATE OF CONTRACT OR ORDER
Merwin & Bray New York	4/9/63	1 Henry Rifle		$42.00	Purchase
New Haven Arms Co., New Haven Connecticut	7/23/63	241 Henry Patent Rifles	$36.00	$8,676.00	6/16 & 6/20/63
	9/19/63	1 Henry Patent Rifle		$44.00	Purchase
	10/31/63	60 Henry Patent Rifles	$36.00	$2,160.00	Purchase
	3/9/64	800 Henry Patent Rifles	$36.00	$28,800.00	12/30/63
	6/17/64	1 Henry Patent Rifle		$40.00	Purchase
	4/19/65	500 Henry Patent Rifles	$38.00	$19,000.00	4/7/65
	5/23/65	127 Henry Patent Rifles	$38.00	$4, 826.00	5/16/65
TOTAL		**1,731 Henry Rifles**		**$63,588.00**	

forty-three and one-half inches and weigh nine pounds four ounces. The twenty-four inch, blue octagonal barrel has a low blade front sight and a folding-leaf sliding rear sight. The majority of the rear sights are found forward of the receiver while a few are mounted on the receiver. The top of the barrel is marked in two lines:

HENRY'S PATENT. OCT. 16, 1860

MANUFACT'D BY THE NEW HAVEN ARMS CO. NEW HAVEN, CT.

The serial number is found located between the rear sight and the frame. A four-piece hickory cleaning rod was stored in the black walnut buttstock. Henry rifles were not equipped with a forearm.

In the 1863-1864 Ordnance Department survey of small arms in field usage, seven officers from the lst District of Columbia Cavalry commented on the Henry rifle. Out of the seven officers, six considered it the best arm in the service while the other officer considered it as a very good arm. Lieutenant W.S. Coner, commented, *"that they carry well, do not get out of order easily, that the lever and spiral spring breaks most often, that he prefers small calibers and considers it the best arm in the service."*[15]

While many regiments were issued a few Henry rifles, only the lst District of Columbia Cavalry was completely armed with the them.

On March 31, 1864, they were issued seven hundred eighty-three Henry rifles and three months later, on June 30, an additional six hundred thirty-nine were delivered.[16] Major Joel W. Cloudman had this to say, *"On the 25th day of August, 1864, near Ream's Station, we had an opportunity of testing the rifle. Our Regiment of Cavalry was dismounted at 4 o'clock, P.M., marched and stationed on the extreme left of the infantry line, there to build light breastworks for the moment. There we received a most desperate charge from the enemy. We used the Henry rifles and easily repulsed the foe, while the infantry were broken and swept from their well constructed breastworks. Our Regiment with the Henry rifle stood like veterans, and never left the line until the battle ceased. Our men often said, and I concur in the opinion, that with this rifle and plenty of ammunition they could safely meet four to one men with any other arm."*[17]

Several of this regiments' Henry rifles were captured by the 7th Virginia Cavalry at Stony Creek, Virginia on June 24, 1864 and later used by them at Ream's Station on August 24 against Union General Hancock's II Infantry Corps. An additional two hundred Henrys were taken at Sycamore Church on September 15th from the

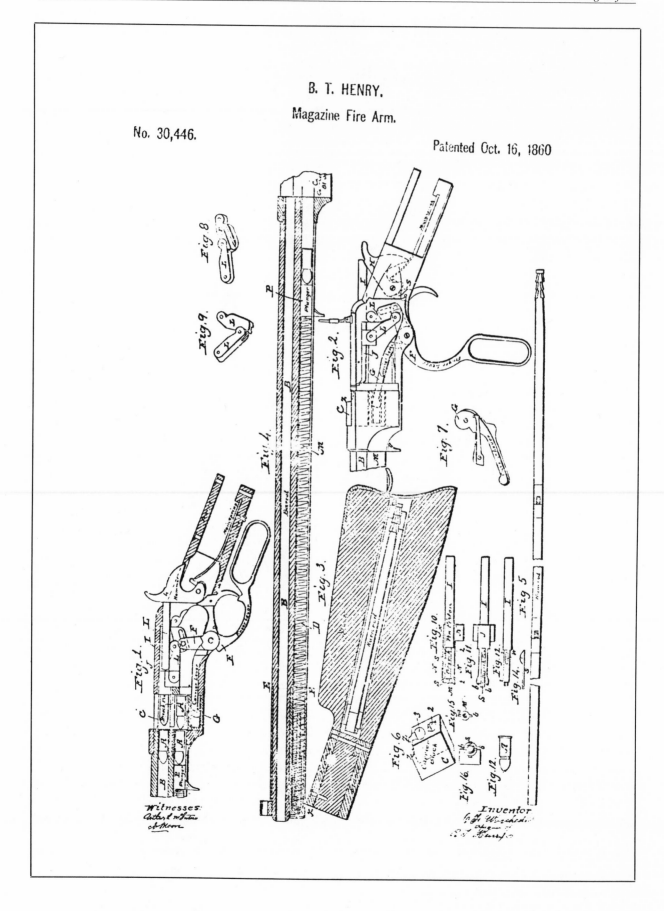

B. T. HENRY.

Magazine Fire Arm.

No. 30,446.

Patented Oct. 16, 1860

lst D.C. Cavalry. These captured Henrys were issued to the 7th, llth, 12th and 35th Virginia Cavalry. The Henry rifles were also in the hands of Captain Jesse McNeill's Rangers when they captured Union Major Generals George Crook and Benjamin F. Kelley on February 21, 1865 at Cumberland, Maryland.[18]

A partial list of Federal regiments which were issued Henry rifles includes the lst Maine, 12th Kentucky and lst District of Columbia Cavalry plus the 7th, 16th, 23rd, 51st, 66th, 80th Illinois and the 58th, 93rd, and 97th Indiana as well as the 7th West Virginia Infantry.

In 1866 the New Haven Arms Company was renamed the Winchester Repeating Arms Company. The firm continued manufacturing the Henry through 1866 with a total production of between thirteen thousand five hundred ane fourteen thousand rifles. In 1867 the first of the Model 1866 Winchester was manufactured which had the King's improvements of a spring-closed loading gate in the frame and an enclosed magazine. These were major improvements over the Henry in that it corrected the open slot in the magazine which permitted the spring to become foul with sand and mud and render the rifle unserviceable.

During the post war years of 1866-1873, the U.S. Cavalry was armed with both Spencer and 50/70 Sharps carbines. With no further need for the Henry rifles, the Government offered them for sale on the open market. On November 22, 1866 at Fort Monroe depot, twenty-four Henrys were sold for prices ranging from $2.25 to $14.50 each.[19] Fifty-seven Henry rifles were sold in Washington, D.C. on June 2, 1868 for $7.62 each to Charles Fritscru[20] and as late as June 1871, the St. Louis Arsenal was selling seven Henry rifles for $6.25 each.[21] In addition, eight hundred eight Henry rifles were taken home by the soldiers in June of 1865.[22]

Rich and famous, B. Tyler Henry retired and moved to New Hampshire where he died in 1898. His rifle was one of the first truly successful repeaters and with his rimfire cartridge, helped the future success of these firearms.

---

[1]L.D. Satterlee, *Henry's Repeating Rifle,* 10 Old Gun Catalogs, Chicago, 1962, P. 8.

[2]U.S. Patent Office, U.S. Patent No. 30,446 of October 16, 1860

[3]ibid.

[4]National Archives Record Group 156-994.

[5]ibid.

[6]Satterlee, op. cit. p. 31.

[7]ibid.

[8]National Archives Record Group 74-145.

[9]Satterlee, op. cit. p. 27.

[10]Executive document No. 99, 40th Congress, 2nd Session.

[11]ibid.

[12]ibid.

[13]ibid.

[14]ibid.

[15]National Archives Record Group 156-215.

[16]National Archives Record Group 156-110.

[17]Satterlee, op. cit. p. 7

[18]Wayne R. Austerman, *Virginia Cavalcade, Winter 1985,* pp. 104-107.

[19]National Archives Record Group 156-125.

[20]National Archives Record Group 156-124.

[21]National Archives Record Group 156-125.

[22]Frances A. Lord, *They Fought for the Union,* Harrisburg, 1960, p. 166.

[23]Executive Document No. 99, 40th Congress, 2nd Session.

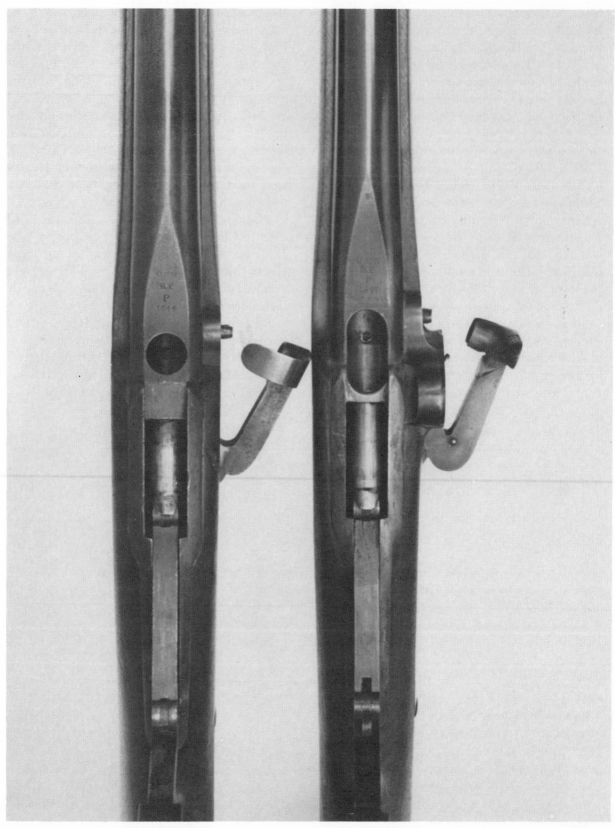

Close-up of the round and oval loading apertures of the Jenks breech loader. The Ames-made rifle on the left exhibits the 'mule ear' side hammer commonly associated with this weapon. The Remington manufactured Jenks carbine on the right shows the later modified 'mule ear' hammer and the Maynard Tape Primer.
                                                                                     — Ralph E. Arnold collection

THE JENKS NAVY RIFLE

The Jenks rifles and carbines have the distinction of being the second breech loaders adopted by the United States. They are also the only arm adopted by the Government to use the 'mule-ear' side hammer and have the percussion nipple going through the lockplate.

These streamlined rifles were the invention of William Jenks of Columbia, South Carolina. His breechloaders were covered by U.S. Patent No. 747 of May 25, 1838 which stated in part:

"Be it known that I, WILLIAM JENKS, of Columbia, in the district of Richland and State of South Carolina, have invented an Improvement in the Manner of Constructing Fire-Arms of Various Kinds; and I do hereby declare that the following is a full and exact description thereof.

My improvement consists in a new mode of constructing such fire-arms as are made to load at the breech, and the accompanying drawings represent it as applied to a rifle, common gun, or fire-arms in general, the general construction being the same with whatever kind of fire-arms it may be used."[1]

The sliding breech-bolt which was the result of this patent worked as follows: The loading lever is raised upward which draws the sliding breech-bolt rearward. This motion exposes the oval loading aperture for inserting of the loose powder and ball. The lowering of the lever drives the breech-bolt forward and sets the powder charge forward into the chamber. Jenks patent claim read:

"What I claim as of my invention, and desire to secure by Letters Patent, is;

The combination of the slide, plug, and stop, operating and constructed substantially in the manner and for the purpose herein set forth."[2]

After receiving his patent in 1838, William Jenks moved from South Carolina to Remington's Corner, Herkimer County, New York. Here he became the neighbor of Eliphalet Remington, the founder of the firm E. Remington & Sons.

Between July 16, 1838 and January 16, 1839, Jenks had his flint-lock carbine tested by a Board of Officers at Watervliet Arsenal. The board was to examine the Jenks system for possible adoption for federal service. During these test trials, William Jenks personally fired one of his carbines first at a rate of seven rounds in three minutes and in the second attempt completed only eleven shots in five and one-half minutes.[3] This rate of fire was not a general improvement over the flint-lock muzzleloading rifle and was, therefore, found unsuited for service use.

Being unmoved by the Board's results, Jenks went to Chicopee Falls, Massachusetts to have a number of his guns manufactured at the Chicopee Falls Company. In 1839, the Government ordered one hundred of the Jenks flint-lock carbines. Carlisle Barracks received twenty-five of these carbines and a like number were sent to Florida for issue to the Second Dragoons who were fighting the Seminole Indians. These carbines were not looked upon with favor by either Captain Sumner at Carlisle or Captain Bradford in Florida. They were, therefore, sent to storage at the Springfield Armory. In December of 1843, sixty-five of these Jenks carbines were converted to percussion at a cost of $3.50 each. The total expense to the Government for this conversion amounted to $227.50.[4] These conversions were made by Major James Ripley at the Springfield Armory.

Turning to the more commonly found percussion Jenks, we find that they are equipped with the unique 'mule-ear' side hammer. This

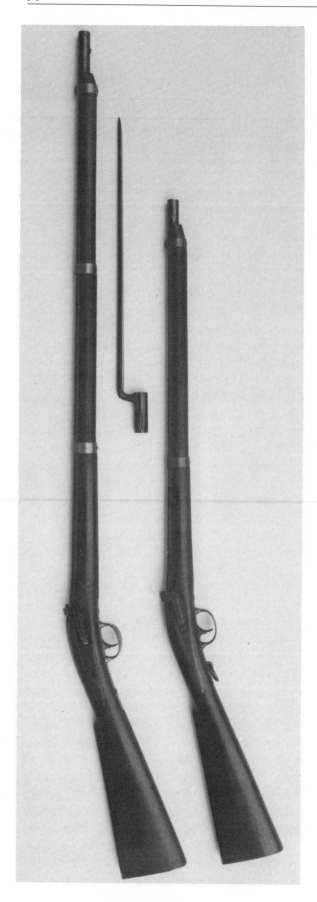

Comparison of the two Jenks breech loaders delivered under the contract of September 2, 1841. The agreement called for 1,000 36" barrel carbines (i.e. rifles) equipped with bayonets and 500 24" barrel carbines, all to be delivered to the Philadelphia Navy Yard before the end of August, 1842.   — Ralph E. Arnold collection

side-striking hammer is curved at its top edge which serves to hold the breech closed. To operate the 'mule-ear' hammer, it is pulled sideways to the right which allows the capping of the nipple for firing of the rifle.

The first of the percussion Jenks' contracts to be entered into between William Jenks and the Board of Navy Commissioners (United States Navy Department) is dated August 30, 1841 at Philadelphia, Pennsylvania. It was not signed, however, by the contracting parties until September 2. This contract called for Jenks to manufacture and deliver at his own risk one thousand five hundred carbines to the Philadelphia Navy Yard. One thousand of these carbines were to have thirty-six inch barrels equipped with a bayonet having a seventeen inch blade. The stipulated price to be paid was $19 each. The remaining five hundred carbines were to have twenty-four inch barrels and cost $18 each.[5] The appendages included with the September 2 order were one cone key, one two-cavity bullet mold and one iron ramrod for every ten carbines plus one screwdriver for each carbine. The contract called for the entire lot of one thousand five hundred carbines and appendages to be delivered at the Navy Yard within one year or by August 30, 1842.[6]

The thirty-six inch barrel carbines called for in the August 30, 1841 contract are generally considered to be more appropriately classified as rifles — hence the term 'Navy rifle' covered by this chapter.

The manufacturer of these Jenks Navy rifles and the five hundred twenty-four inch barrel carbines was Nathan P. Ames, Jr. (1803-1847). Nathan and his brother, James T. Ames (1810-1883) had formed the Ames Manufacturing Company in 1834 at Cabotville, Massachusetts. Though they were the major supplier of swords to the government, this was a new experience — manufacturing firearms for the U.S. Navy. To meet the expansion requirements of the business brought on by the naval contract, the Ames Manufacturing Company purchased,

This rare Naval powder flask, decorated with a fouled anchor, was manufactured by George Adams and was used with both the 36″ barrel and 24″ barrel versions of the Jenks 'carbine'. The non-adjustable spout dispensed 65 grains of powder and the flask held approximately 14 ounces. — Ralph E. Arnold collection

in 1841, the operations of the Chicopee Falls Company and it was from these new facilities that the Jenks contract of 1841 was fulfilled.

Many months passed before the Ames factory was ready for proof testing a portion of the carbine barrels. Finally, on July 8, 1842, Jenks wrote to Commander Lewis Warrington that three hundred barrels were ready for proof testing and inspection. A week later, on July 15, Commander Warrington requested from the U.S. Ordnance Office in Washington the services of an army inspector to inspect the Jenks barrels. For this task, the Army sent Captain W.A. Thornton of the New York City Ordnance Depot.[7]

The proof testing of these barrels took several weeks and, therefore, on August 22 Nathan Ames wrote the Navy requesting additional time to make deliveries on his contract, due to expire on August 30. The Navy agreed and replied on September 8 that a reasonable extension of time would be given.

Additional time would be needed before the initial two hundred carbines were received by the Boston Navy Yard in May of 1843.[8] On August 25 Captain Thornton notified the Navy that the last three hundred of the twenty-four inch barrel carbines had been inspected and were available for delivery.

In Captain Thornton's letter of August 25, he also stated that Ames was in the process of starting the manufacturing of the thirty-six inch barrel rifles. The initial deliveries of these rifles were received at Boston in December when the last three hundred carbines and the first two hundred rifles were accepted. The next delivery of rifles was in May of 1844 when one hundred were delivered. The last of these rifles were finally received in December of 1844. These rifles were packed twenty to a crate, the crates costing the government $3.85 each.[9]

The September 2, 1841 contract was the only agreement entered into with the Navy Department to specify the thirty-six inch barrel. These 'mule-ear' Jenks rifles are found in .52

caliber smoothbore and rifled in .54 caliber. The overall length of this rifle is fifty-two and one-half inches long and weighs six pounds twelve ounces. The full length black walnut stock is forty-nine and one-half inches in length. The casehardened lockplate is marked N.P. AMES/ SPRINGFIELD/MASS and at the rear of the plate Wm JENKS. The thirty-five and three-eighths inch brown barrel is stamped at the rear Wm JENKS/USN/ Initial of Inspectors JL & RP for Joseph Lanaman and Richard Paine/P/ date such as 1844. The bayonet stud is under the barrel near the muzzle. The brown triangular bayonet is marked USN. The Jenks rifle has three brass barrel bands. The upper band supports an integral front sight while the rearsight is

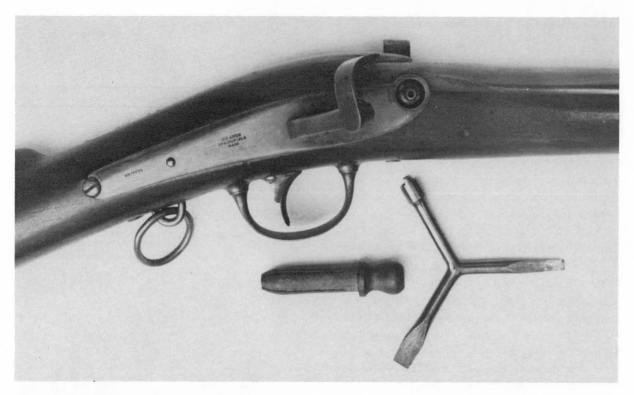

Close-up of the Jenks lock manufactured by N.P. Ames. Note that the percussion nipple is mounted through the lockplate. these 'mule ear' side hammer Jenks were the only such arms purchased the the United States. Also pictured here is a rare Jenks combination tool and tompion in .52 caliber.   — Ralph E. Arnold collection

a 'V' groove on the top of the operating lever. All furniture is brass.

The fouled anchor navy powder flasks used with the Jenks have a spout which dispenses sixty-five grains of powder. These flasks, which hold up to fourteen ounces of powder, were manufactured by George Adams, N.P. Ames and George Stimpson.

The bullet moulds made for the Jenks, specified in the September 2, 1841 contract, had two cavities which produced round balls .525 inches in diameter and weighing approximately two hundred nineteen grains.

While the August 30, 1841 contract was the only one calling for the Jenks Navy rifle, more Jenks carbines were manufactured by Ames for the U.S. Navy, eventually totaling four thousand two hundred between 1841-1845. In addition, forty Jenks carbines were delivered to the Army on January 23, 1844 and issued to Companies 'D' and 'E' of the First Dragoons.

September 22, 1845 saw William Jenks enter into a contract with the Bureau of Ordnance and Hydrography for one thousand carbines equipped with the Maynard tape priming device. These carbines were manufactured by E. Remington & Son in 1846-47.

In 1858, James Merrill of Baltimore, Maryland received U.S. Patent No. 20,954 of July 20 which allowed the Jenks to be altered to his breechloading design. Merrill's system allowed the Jenks to use a combustible cartridge instead of loose ball and powder. Three hundred of these altered Jenks were delivered to the Ordnance Department in September 1860.

At the outbreak of the Civil War many of the Jenks were still in active naval service. On May 13, 1861, thirty thousand Jenks cartridges were sent from the Washington Navy Yards to New York.[10] However, as more effective small arms were obtained by the Navy, they started to replace the Jenks which were being turned back in to the Ordnance Depots. In a letter written by Captain Andrew Harwood, Chief of Naval Ordnance, to the Boston Navy Yard on June 14, he ordered that the Jenks be replaced by the Sharps rifles aboard all vessels then being fitted out of Portsmouth for sea duty.[11] As the 'St. Lawrence' was being fitted out for sea duty at the Philadelphia Navy Yard, the Jenks was also

GOVERNMENT PROCUREMENT OF JENKS RIFLES[17]

CONTRACTOR'S OR SELLER'S NAME	DATE OF PURCHASE	QUANTITY OR KIND OF STORES	PRICE	AMOUNT	DATE OF CONTRACT OR ORDER
N.P. Ames	12/43	200 Jenks Rifles & Bayonets	$19.00	$3,800.00	9/2/41
	5/44	100 Jenks Rifles & Bayonets	$19.00	$1,900.00	9/2/41
	7/44	500 Jenks Rifles & Bayonets	$19.00	$9,500.00	9/2/41
	12/44	200 Jenks Rifles & Bayonets	$19.00	$3,800.00	9/2/41
TOTAL		**1000 Jenks Rifles**		**$19,000.00**	

replaced with Sharps rifles.[12]

In the early days of the war, a number of Jenks carbines were salvaged from the *USS Pennsylvania* by the Confederates when they captured the Norfolk Navy Yard. In May of 1861, these captured arms were issued to the 2nd Virginia Cavalry Battalion.[13]

Finding the smoothbore Jenks carbines obsolete for further U.S. Naval service, Harwood instructed Dahlgren to sell them. In the meantime, Harwood contacted A.M. Eastman of Manchester, New Hampshire, asking if he would be interested in purchasing the obsolete Jenks. After a couple of weeks consideration, Eastman offered the Navy $3 each for the old carbines. In August of 1861 two thousand eight hundred Jenks of both the twenty-four and thirty-six inch barrel varieties were sold to Eastman who immediately turned them over to W.W. Marston of New York City who had been employed to rifle them.[14]

In addition to rifling, the twenty-four inch barrel carbines were fitted with sling swivel rings suggesting they were not intended to be sold back to the Navy. Sometime after October 1861, they were sold on the open market — to whom remains unknown.

It is noteworthy that while Eastman was purchasing the Jenks from the Navy Department, he also purchased five thousand Model 1843 Hall carbines from the Ordnance Department. Obtained at a cost of $3.50 each, and after being rifled for an additional $1 per carbine, the Hall's were sold back to the government through General Fremont for $22 each.

Even after selling the two thousand eight hundred carbines to Eastman, a number of Jenks still remained in the various navy yards. On October 18, 1862, Dahlgren authorized the Boston Navy Yards to sell at the next auction all Jenks carbines presently being stored there.[15] A number of Jenks still remained in Naval Storage throughout the war, and as late as December 1, 1866, one hundred seven were still in service with thirty-two at the Philadelphia Navy Yard, fifty-six at New York and nineteen at Norfolk.[16]

[1] *U.S. Patent Office, U.S. Patent No. 747, May 25, 1838.*
[2] *Ibid.*
[3] *Andrew F. Lustyik, The Jenks Carbine* (Part I), The Gun Report, July 1964, p. 8.
[4] Ibid, p. 10.
[5] Ibid, p. 11.
[6] Ibid.
[7] Andrew F. Lustyik, *The Jenks Carbine* (Part II), The Gun Report, August 1864, p. 19.
[8] NARG 74, Section 157.
[9] Ibid.
[10] NARG 74-6.
[11] Ibid.
[12] Ibid.
[13] Frederick P. Todd, *American Military Equipage 1851-1872 Volume II State Forces,* Chatham Squire Press, Inc., 1983, p. 1272.
[14] Joint Committee on the Conduct of the War, Congressional Serial Set No. 1142, p. 238.
[15] NARG 74-3.
[16] H. R. Executive Document No. 16-2, 39th Congress (Dec. 31, 1866).
[17] NARG 74, Section 157.

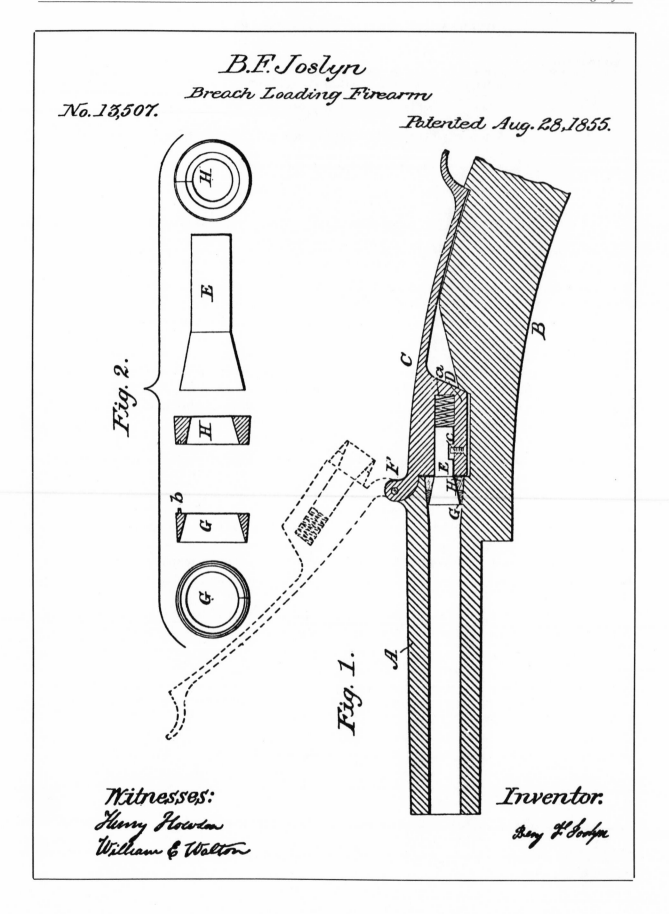

B. F. Joslyn

Breach Loading Firearm

No. 13,507.

Patented Aug. 28, 1855.

Fig. 2.

Fig. 1.

Witnesses:

Henry Howden

William E. Walton

Inventor.

Benj. F. Joslyn

THE M1855 JOSLYN RIFLE

One of the rarest breech-loading rifles to be manufactured during the Civil War was the .58 caliber percussion Joslyn rifle. It is also known as the Model 1855 for the year in which the patent was issued.

The inventor, Benjamin F. Joslyn, of Worcester, Massachusetts, is believed to have been born in 1821. Little is known of his early life, however, we do know that on December 21, 1847 he was united in marriage to Almira H. Clements of Worcester. At the time of his 1855 patent, he is listed in the Worcester directory as a partner with John P. Marshall in the manufacturing of improved firearms. Their business address was listed on Armory Street.

On August 28, 1855, Joslyn was granted U.S. Patent No. 13,507 for his design which was to cover both his percussion carbines and rifles. He states in his patent:

'This invention relates to fire-arms which are loaded at the breech; and it consists in furnishing the radial or hinged breech with a pin which, is allowed to have a longitudinal movement against a spring in the said breech, but is prevented from turning therein. This pin has a conical head embraced by metallic expanding rings, which, when the radial breech is down and the cartridge inserted, penetrate a slight distance into and fit against the interior of the barrel, the cartridge bearing directly against the end of the pin, so that when the powder is ignited the sudden expansion of gas drives the pin toward the interior of the radial breech, the cone end at the same time causing the rings to expand and fit tight to the interior of the barrel, thus rendering the latter air and gas tight at the breech and causing the explosive force to be more efficient.'[1]

Joslyn's first attempt to interest the government in his percussion breech-loading design was with his carbine. On August 10, 1857, William C. Freeman of 115 Nassau Street, New York City, acting as agent for Joslyn, wrote to the Ordnance Office offering to present a carbine for the 1857 Breech-Loading Trials held at West Point. This trial board found that the Joslyn carbine submitted by Freeman was very effective at one hundred yards but ineffective at six hundred yards. All parts of the carbine worked well with no gas leaks. Particles of powder did, however, get into the joint and caused great difficulty in closing the breech completely.

Finding the overall results favorable, Freeman requested, on November 23, 1857, that the government purchase a number of Joslyn carbines for further tests. An order was placed by the Secretary of War for fifty carbines at $35 each. The delivery of these carbines was completed on November 15, 1858 when they were shipped from the A.H. Waters Armory of Millbury, Massachusetts to St. Louis.

The following year, 1859, found the Navy also interested in the Joslyn design. Needing small arms for their marine guards aboard ships and for ship boarding parties, the Navy found that the rifle was more effective for their service needs, and therefore, was interested in obtaining Joslyn rifles.

On August 9, 1859, the Navy wrote William Freeman to inquire at what price would he furnish them with five hundred of Joslyn's breech-loading rifles. These rifles were to have thirty inch barrels and be in .58 caliber.[2] This letter was followed up on September 6 when they again wrote Freeman stating that the Sharps Rifle Manufacturing Company would furnish their Sharps rifle with sword bayonet for $37.50 each and inquired if the Joslyn rifle could be delivered at the same price.

Three days later, on September 9, a con-

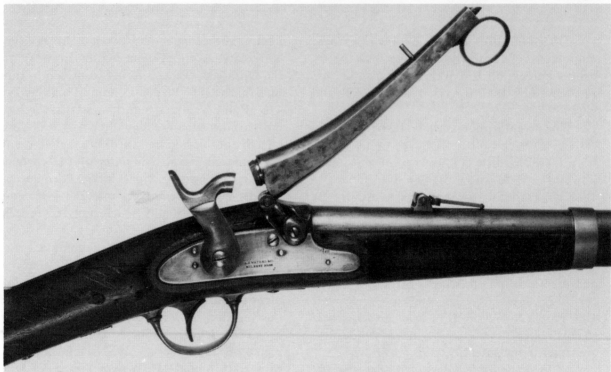

(above) On September 9, 1859, the Navy Ordnance Department placed an order for 500 of these .58 caliber M1855 Joslyn rifles. Disputes over the failure of the contractor to deliver on time caused the Ordnance Department to refuse acceptance of the Joslyn rifles and later to relent and accept an unknown, but almost certainly smaller, quantity of them — perhaps all that were actually manufactured. (below) Close-up view of the breech and rear sight of the Joslyn Navy rifle.   George D. Moller collection

tract was entered into between the Navy and Freeman, which stated in part:

'The bureau will receive from you to be delivered at the Navy Yards - Washington within four months from this date 500 of Joslyn's breech-loading guns and sword bayonets and scabbards, screwdriver, cone wrench, cartridge stick and extra cone for each gun and one bullet mould to cast six balls for each 25 guns -the caliber to be 0.58 and the length of barrel 30 inches.'[3]

The price was set at $37.50 each or a total cost to the Navy of $18,750 if and when they were delivered.[4]

The January 9, 1860 delivery date on this order came and went without any deliveries

being made. Waiting an additional six months and still receiving no deliveries prompted the Navy on June 8 to write to Freeman requesting an explanation for the delay and when could they expect delivery on the September 9 contract.

While Freeman's response has not been uncovered in the National Archives, the Navy's follow-up correspondence would indicate that Freeman told them that the Joslyn rifles were being manufactured by A.H. Waters of Millbury, Massachusetts under subcontract for him. This did not set well with the Navy, for on June 15 they wrote Freeman stating that it was the Navy's impression that when the September 9 contract was entered into that he would be shortly putting into operation his own factory for the production of this contract. The letter continues by stating that the contract must be fulfilled by the contracting parties (Freeman), and they would not accept deliveries from anyone else.[5]

A few Joslyn rifles eventually were delivered to the Navy — exactly when is not known. It is known that Freeman delivered a few hundred Joslyn carbines to the Ordnance Department in the fall of 1860 and the spring of 1861. It is probably about this time that the Navy received their rifles. The actual number received was likely not more than two hundred. Why the Navy waived their earlier requirement that the rifles be manufactured by Freeman and not Waters can be attributed to the critical shortage of breech-loading rifles available for naval service at the outbreak of the war.

By early 1862 a few of these Joslyn rifles were aboard Captain David G. Farragut's fleet of vessels which captured, in May, the South's second largest city, New Orleans, Lousiana.

Turning to the rifle itself, we find that it was .58 caliber rifled with three grooves. The thirty inch barrel may be found browned or with a blue finish. It has a steel blade front sight and folding leaf, sliding bar rear sight graduated to eight hundred yards. A lug for attaching a sabre bayonet is located on the right side of the barrel four and one-quarter inches from the muzzle.

The overall length of the Joslyn rifle is forty-five and three-quarter inches and it weighs seven pounds fourteen ounces. The barrel is held to the black walnut stock with a single flat brass barrel band. All furniture is brass and there are no sling swivels. The case hardened lockplate is marked forward of the hammer A.H. Waters & Co/MILBURY MASS. Some breech levers are marked with Joslyn's patent date of PATD BY/B.F. JOSLYN/AUG. 28, 1855. The serial number is marked on the left side of the lever.

The number of Joslyn percussion rifles manufactured is believed to be a few hundred at best and probably less. They are found in the same serial range with the percussion carbine. The total of all percussion Joslyn firearms was about one thousand five hundred.

While the rifle was of little success, Joslyn carbines were to fare a little better with the government. During the first two years of the war, the Ordnance Department purchased one thousand sixty of Joslyn's percussion carbines and between 1863 and 1865 obtained another ten thousand two hundred one of his rimfire Model 1862 and 1864 carbines. In total, the Ordnance Department purchased eleven thousand two hundred sixty-one Joslyn carbines plus one thousand one hundred percussion Joslyn revolvers.[6] In addition, the Navy purchased one hundred Joslyn revolvers in 1861.

As late as December 1, 1866 the Navy still had six of the Joslyn rifles in storage, with one at the Philadelphia Naval Yard and five at the New York Navy Yard.[7]

After the war, Benjamin Joslyn moved from Stonington, Connecticut to New York City where he continued his work in the field of firearms. In 1870 he patented a bolt-action system which was promoted by Henry Tomes of New York City. This system was a failure in the 1872 government Breech-Loading Trials and scored, therefore, no commercial success. Between 1855 and 1879, Joslyn received approximately two dozen patents for a variety of firearm designs.

By 1874, Joslyn had moved back to Worcester, Massachusetts and was listed as residing at 29 Clifton Street until 1885.

---

[1]U.S. Patent Office, U.S. Patent No. 13,507 of August 28, 1855.
[2]NARG 74-5.
[3]Ibid.
[4]NARG 74-157.
[5]NARG 74-5.
[6]John D. McAulay, *Carbines of the Civil War 1861-1865,* Union City, 1981, p. 75.
[7]H.R. Executive Document No. 16-2, 38th Congress (Dec. 31, 1866).

J. H. MERRILL.
Breech-Loading Fire-Arm.

No. 20,954.   Patented July 20, 1858

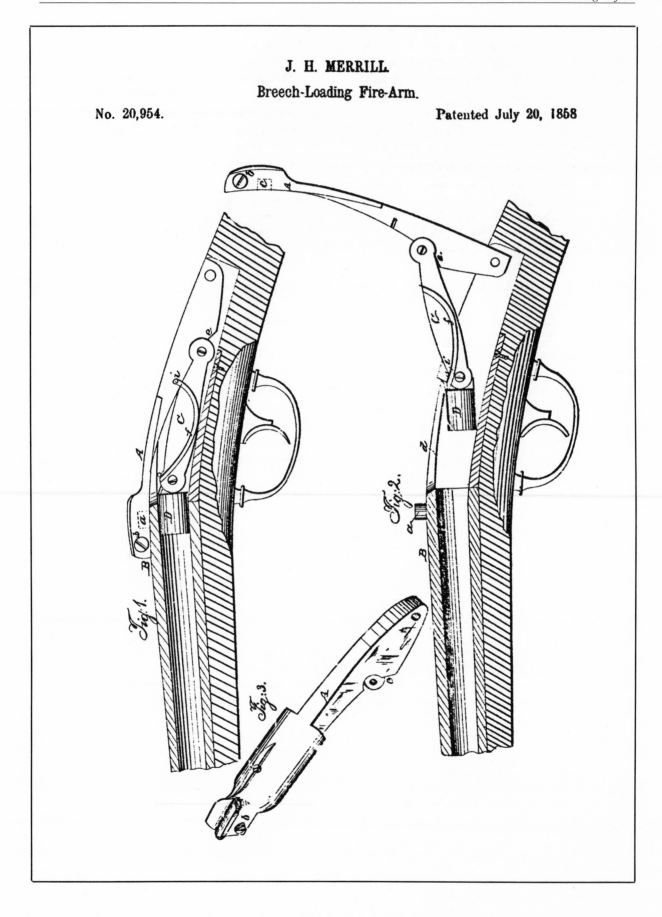

THE MERRILL RIFLE

James H. Merrill of Baltimore, Maryland had been manufacturing small arms since about 1840. In 1855, he became associated with Messrs. Latrobe and Thomas in the firm of Merrill, Latrobe & Thomas.

On July 26, 1855, the Ordnance Department purchased from Merrill, Latrobe & Thomas, one hundred seventy carbines at $35.00 each. These carbines were manufactured on contract by E. Remington & Sons of Ilion, New York. In actual use, these carbines covered by U.S. Patent No. 14,077 of January 8, 1856 were found to be unfit for service and no further orders were forthcoming.

In 1858, Merrill turned his attention to the alteration of the 'Jenks Gun'. To cover this alteration, James Merrill received U.S. Patent No. 20,954 on July 20, 1858. This system allowed the Jenks to use combustible cartridges instead of loose ball and powder. Merrill's actual patent claim read:

'What I claim therein as new, and desire to secure by Letters Patent, is —

Converting what is known as the 'Jenks Carbine' from a loose powder and ball loader to a cartridge loader — viz., by plugging up the vertical opening through which that gun was loaded, cutting away in rear of the barrel so as to load at the rear end of the bore, and allowing the lever, toggle, and piston to come far enough back to admit a cartridge to be dropped in behind the bore and then run up into the chamber, with a groove and pin to guide the toggle and piston, as herein set forth.'[1]

September of 1860 saw three hundred of these altered Jenks carbines delivered to the Ordnance Department. The lever springs were found to be too weak for service use and, therefore, returned to Merrill for further modifications. In addition to the above Jenks carbines,

Merrill also altered a number of M1841 and 1842 rifles and muskets to this system.

About 1860, Latrobe dropped out of the firm and his place was taken by L.W. Thomas. The business now known as Merrill, Thomas & Company was located at 239 Baltimore Street, Baltimore, Maryland.

While the July 20, 1858 patent covered the basic design of Merrill's Civil War carbines and rifles, designer refinements were patented with U.S. Patents No. 32,032 and No. 32,033 of April 9, 1861, No. 32,451 of May 28, 1861, and No. 33,536 of October 22, 1861. The April 9 Patent No. 32,033 was typical of these. Its claim read:

'Having thus fully described the nature and object of my invention, what I claim therein as new is —

1. In Combination with the lever by which the breech is opened and closed, a projection upon or over which the hammer rests when down upon the nipple, to prevent said lever from rising or opening the breech accidentally, substantially as described.

2. In combination with the lever by which the breech of the gun is opened and closed, a projection which extends under the cap when on the nipple, so that the raising of said lever preparatory to recharging the gun shall throw off the exploded cap and leave the nipple free for a fresh cap, substantially as described.'[2]

To operate these Civil War Merrills, first the hammer must be set at the safety position. The flat knurled lever latch (First Model) or the button type lever latch (Second Model) is then drawn to the rear which allows the top lever to be pulled back and upward; this operation draws the breech bolt to the rear to expose the chamber for inserting the paper cartridge. The lever is then returned to the closed position and the rifle is ready for firing with a conventional

J. H. MERRILL.
BREECH LOADING FIREARM.

No. 32,033.   Patented Apr. 9, 1861.

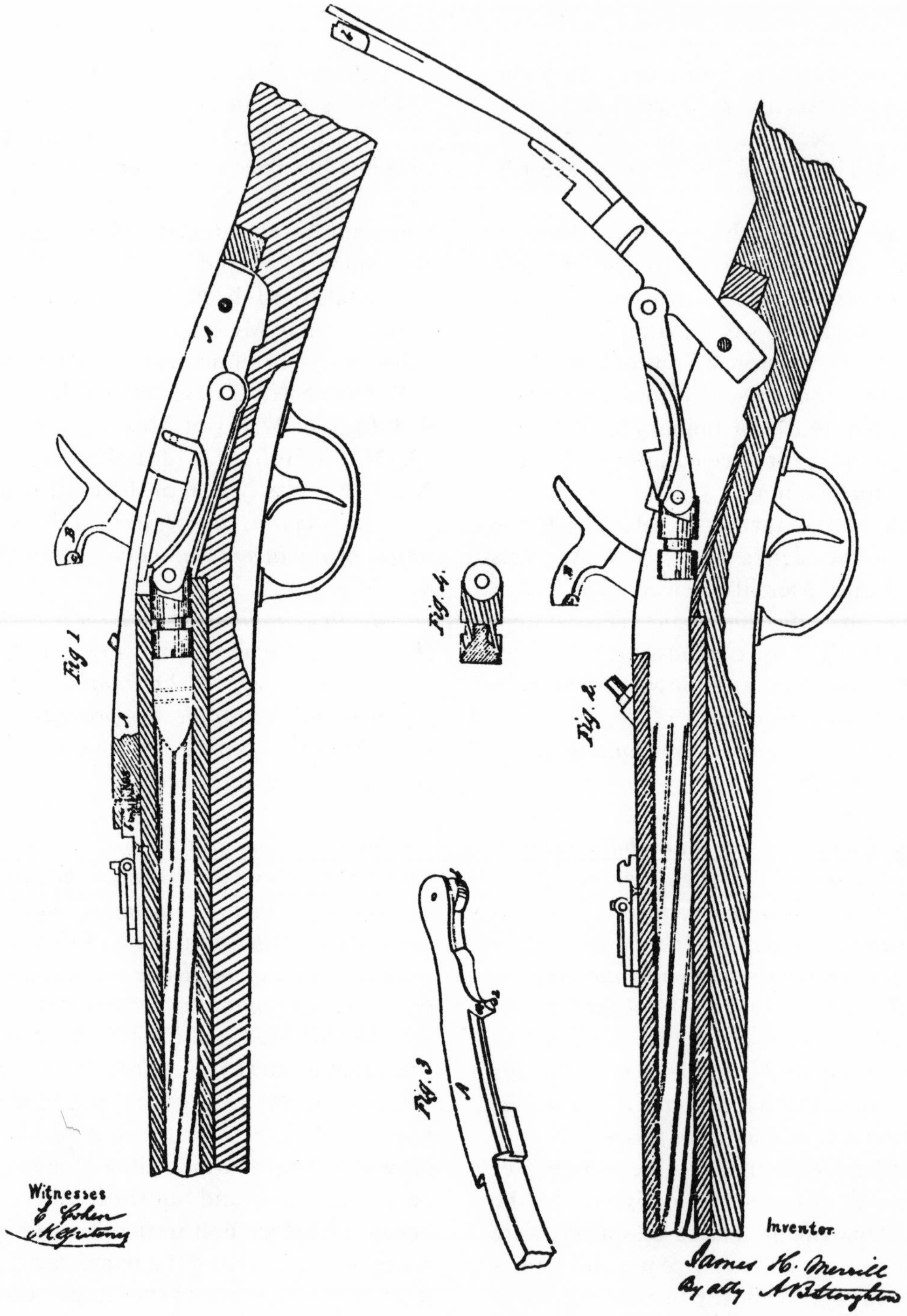

Fig. 1

Fig. 4.

Fig. 2.

Fig. 3.

Witnesses

Inventor.

James H. Merrill
By atty. A. Billington

percussion cap.

Two months after the outbreak of the War in April of 1861, Merrill's agent, S. P. Dinsmore with offices at the Clay Hotel in Washington, D.C. made his first wartime sale to the Ordnance Department on June 5. This sale to the government consisted of twenty Merrill carbines at $25.00 each; one Merrill minie musket at $35.00; three Remington-Merrill carbines at $35.00 each; three Merrill rifles at $35.00 each; and nine Harpers Ferry rifles altered to the Merrill design at $35.00 each. The total of this sale came to $1,260.00.[3]

A price list of August 11, 1861 from Dinsmore to the Ordnance Department set the price for the Merrill carbine at $32.50. The list goes on to give the following information for the Merrill Rifle:

Weight of Rifle	9 pounds 3 ounces
Caliber	.54
No. of Grooves	7
Depth of Grooves	1/100 inch
Twist of Rifling	1 turn in 69¼ inches
Weight of Bullet	410 grains
Powder Charge	50-60 grains
Sales Price	$40.00[4]

Merrill, Thomas & Company's first contract with the Ordnance Department was entered into on October 25, 1861 when six hundred carbines were purchased at a cost of $18,000. The next contract with the Ordnance Office was made on December 24, 1861. This called for the delivery of five thousand breech-loading Merrill carbines and appendages. Deliveries were set at five hundred in thirty days, five hundred more within sixty-five days from December 24 and then one thousand per month.

As deliveries were being made on the December 24 contract, the Ordnance Department on March 22, 1862 requested that five hundred sixty-six Merrill rifles at $45 each including sabre-bayonet, belt, capbox, cartridge box and bayonet scabbard be substituted for the carbine. This request from Ripley reads:

"GENTLEMEN: Be pleased to furnish the 21st regiment Indiana volunteers with 566 Merrill's rifles in place of the same number of Merrill's carbines, which you have contracted to furnish this department. The price to be $45, sabre-bayonet, belt, cap boxes, cartridge boxes, and bayonet scabbard complete, included. These stores should be turned over to Major Belger, United States quartermaster, for transportation to the colonel of the regiment, which, I understand, is at Fort Monroe, Virginia. Be pleased to signify your acceptance of this order."[5]

What led up to this March 22 request for the Merrill rifle for the 21st Indiana Infantry had its beginning the previous December. In December of 1861, Company 'K' commanded by Captain Jacob Hess received their Merrill rifles. These rifles were probably purchased by the state directly from the Merrill Company. Captain Hess' high regard for these rifles can be seen in his letter written to the company.

"GENTLEMEN: My Company having armed themselves with your 'Breech-Loading Infantry Rifle', I challenge the world to compete with them, using any other weapon. A target is placed at the distance of one thousand yards or under is riddled to atoms by a squad of six or eight men at every fire. I have tested the qualities of your Rifle until I am satisfied it merits all the praise bestowed upon it. The facility, rapidity and ease with which it can be used has no equal. The ingenuity and simplicity which celebrated your Gun far supersedes any that has come under my observation. Let the noble men of the gallant Twenty-First sum up their interests as to what they need to sustain their honor in this deplorable war, and equip themselves with the 'Merrill Breech-Loading Rifle', and then they can laugh at opposition.

In conclusion, permit me to say, hope, that you will regard my foregoing recommendation in the same light that it is meant."[6]

Captain Hess's opinion of the Merrill was also shared by Colonel McMillan. He wrote Congressman W. McKee Dun requesting that Dun put pressure on the Secretary of War to have his whole command issued the Merrill rifle. Colonel McMillan's letter of January 22 to Dun reads in part: *"One of my Companies of the 21st Indiana Regiment, having after a full and very satisfactory trial of the 'Merrill Patent Breech-Loading Infantry Rifle,' determined to supply themselves with it, and the result of this more extended use for a month past by this*

Overhead and side views of the Merrill rifle. Note, in the lower photograph, the breech bolt which presses the paper cartridge forward into the chamber with the closing of the action.
                                                                                                Authors' collection

whole Company proving that this arm in actual service is really more simple and efficient in every respect than the muzzleloaders. The entire Regiment have resolved to have them, and accordingly have offered to purchase one thousand from the makers here, proposing to pay for them by assigning fifteen dollars per man out of every pay-roll until the whole cost (forty-five dollars) is paid. This the manufacturers say they are unable to do; I therefore write you, to ask if you will not see the Secretary of War and ascertain if he cannot make an arrangement by which the Government will pay the makers as the arms are delivered, looking to the pay-roll of the men for reimbursement."[7]

The initial delivery of the March 22 request for the Merrill rifles was received by the Government on April 25 when a lot of forty rifles was delivered. It took the remainder of the year before all five hundred sixty-six rifles were received at the Ordnance Department. The last sixty-six rifles on this contract were shipped from the Merrill factory in December of 1862.

The 21st Indiana Infantry was the only regiment to be extensively armed with the Merrill

rifle during the War. Other regiments had a few Merrills issued to individual sharpshooters. The quarterly ordnance reports from the infantry and cavalry regiments show that the largest number of Merrill rifles in service at any one time occurred during the quarter ending June 30, 1864 when the 21st Indiana (lst Heavy Artillery) is listed as having 202 rifles on hand.[8] Other Infantry regiments to have used the Merrill rifles during the War were the 7th and 10th Michigan, 4th Arkansas and the lst Massachusetts Sharpshooters.[9] Cavalry regiments also were issued the Merrill rifle and they are known to have been in use with the 6th Kansas, 3rd Wisconsin and llth Ohio.[10]

In reviewing the history of the 21st Indiana Infantry, we see that it was organized at Indianapolis, Indiana on July 24, 1861. The 21st left Indiana for Baltimore, Maryland on July 31 and were to remain there until March of 1862 when they became part of General Butler's New Orleans Expedition. They were the first regiment to land at New Orleans on May 1. In February of 1863 their designation was changed to the lst Indiana Heavy Artillery. They were on

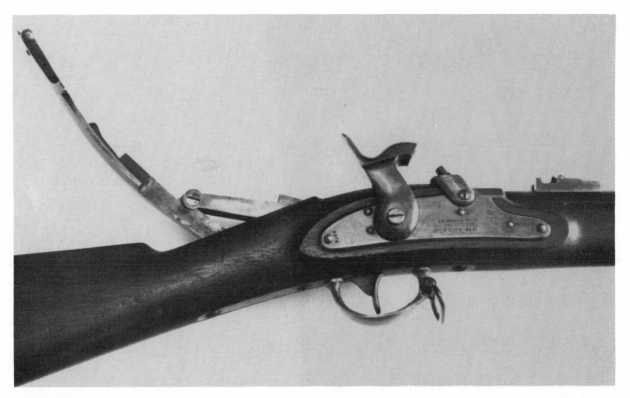

Close-up of the breech section of the Merrill rifle — shown here with the action open. This is a second-type Merrill, with the round button-type lever latch, serial number 8970.   Authors collection

active duty until January 10, 1866 when they were mustered out at Baton Rouge, Louisana.[11]

The only unit at Gettysburg that had Merrill rifles was the lst Massachusetts Sharpshooters. On July 3, Lieutenant L.E. Bicknell's command of twenty men was located between Ziegler's Groove and Emmitsburg Road at the time of Pickett's Charge. They were able to help repulse the attack of A.P. Hill's Infantry during this attack. During the battle, the lst Massachusetts Sharpshooters had two men killed and six wounded.

How were the rifles received by the troops? Lieut. Charles D. Judd, Co. 'F' 2nd N.Y. Artillery wrote:

"On looking over my journal I find that at 750 yards, 86 balls hit the mark out of 100. Size of target, 18 in. x 12 in. At 350 yards, 38 out of 42. At eleven hundred yards, on an average, I did even better than the former, but with a steady rest."[12]

A second comment came from Colonel Samuel Carroll, a brigade commander in Major General Wm. French's Division of the 2nd Army Corps. It is taken from Carroll's Chancel-lorsville battle report of May 3, 1863.

"I found that a 'Merrill Rifle', furnished one of the men by the Division Commander, reached the enemy's sharpshooters when none of our other guns seemed to have any effect on them, and would respectfully request that two Companies of my Brigade by armed with them."[13]

Commissary Sergeant Harding of the 21st Indiana stated that they were accurate to six hundred yards. They were fired as often as eighty times without cleaning and found to be superior to the Sharps. Colonel McMillan, in a letter to the manufacturer, comments:

"The battle of Baton Rouge, gave a good opportunity of thoroughly testing your Breech-Loading Infantry Rifle. I am more thoroughly convinced than ever, that it will be the best gun for Light Infantry in use. My boys having them, fired fifty per cent, more shots than those with the Enfield or Austrian."[14]

On October 10, 1863, Mr. T.E. Thomas, Treasurer of the Merrill Arms Company wrote General Ramsay at the Ordnance Department offering to sell the army two hundred Merrill rifles. This offer was accepted on October 26

GOVERNMENT PROCUREMENT OF MERRILL RIFLES[19]

CONTRACTOR'S OR SELLER'S NAME	DATE OF PURCHASE	QUANTITY OR KIND OF STORES	PRICE	AMOUNT	DATE OF CONTRACT OR ORDER
Merrill, Thomas & Co.	6/5/61	3 Merrill Rifles	$35.00	$105.00	Purchase
	4/25/62	40 Merrill Rifles	$45.00	$1,800.00	12/24/61
	5/29/62	40 Merrill Rifles	$45.00	$1,800.00	12/24/61
	6/19/62	40 Merrill Rifles	$45.00	$1,800.00	12/24/61
	7/7/62	40 Merrill Rifles	$45.00	$1,800.00	12/24/61
	8/62	60 Merrill Rifles	$45.00	$2,700.00	12/24/61
	10/7/62	40 Merrill Rifles	$45.00	$1,800.00	12/24/61
	10/31/62	60 Merrill Rifles	$45.00	$2,700.00	12/24/61
	11/7/62	40 Merrill Rifles	$45.00	$1,800.00	12/24/61
	11/12/62	40 Merrill Rifles	$45.00	$1,800.00	12/24/61
	11/15/62	60 Merrill Rifles	$45.00	$2,700.00	12/24/61
	11/24/62	40 Merrill Rifles	$45.00	$1,800.00	12/24/61
Merrill Patent Firearms Co.	12/62	66 Merrill Rifles	$45.00	$2,970.00	12/24/61
	11/30/63	200 Merrill Rifles	$30.00	$6,000.00	10/26/63
TOTAL		**769 Merrill Rifles**		**$31,000.00**	

when Ramsay wrote Thomas stating that he would pay $30 for each rifle with sabre bayonet. Deliveries were to be made at the Washington Arsenal.

"SIR: Referring to your letter of the 10th instant offering to furnish this department with two hundred Merrill's rifles, with sabre bayonets and accoutrements, I have to state that your offer is accepted, the rifles and accoutrements to be subject to the usual inspection and proof. For each rifle, with sabre bayonet, you will be paid thirty dollars ($30) and for each set of accoutrements three dollars and fifty cents ($3.50) upon the usual certificates of inspection and receipt, in such funds as the Treasury Department may provide. These rifles are to be delivered at the Washington arsenal. Lieutenant Colonel Hagner has been directed to inspect them when notified by you."[15]

These rifles were received on November 30 along with the deliveries of one thousand Mer-

rill carbines. This would bring to a total of seven hundred sixty-nine Merrill rifles plus fourteen thousand two hundred fifty-five carbines purchased by the Ordnance Department during the War at a cost of $105,779.32.[16] In addition, five million five hundred two thousand seven hundred fifty cartridges were obtained.

The wartime Merrill rifles are of .54 caliber with an overall length of forty-eight and one-half inches and weighing nine pounds two ounces. The case-hardened lockplate is marked on the early models: J.H. MERRILL BALTO.-/PAT. JULY 1858/APL 9 MAY 21-28-61. These markings are forward of the hammer and to the rear of the hammer the serial number such as 8970. The later model varies only with a spread eagle forward of the hammer and the date of 1863 to the rear of the hammer. These later dated 1863 were of the October 26, 1863 contract.

The black walnut stock has the inspector's

cartouche on the left side. The inspector's initials of ZB for Zadock Butt are most often encountered.

The thirty-three inch barrel has a lug for a sabre bayonet on the right side. Barrels are found finished either brown or blued. There is an iron blade front sight and a two leaf folding rear sight graduated to five hundred yards which also serves as a catch for the breech lever. There are two types of breech lever latch — the First Model has a knurled breech latch and Second Model a button type plunger latch.

The two barrel bands, trigger guard, butt-plate, and patchbox are usually found made of brass; a few however, are known made of iron. The steel button-head ramrod is invariably found finished bright. Many of the parts were stamped with a batch number such as 0/46. The case-hardened operating lever is marked:

J H MERRILL BALTO/PAT JULY 1858

The serial number is found at the rear of the operating lever. The brass patchbox held a 'U' shaped combination screwdriver and an extra nipple.

The brass handled saber bayonet issued with the Merrill rifle is twenty-four and one-eighth inches long with a nineteen and one-half inch blade. There are no markings on the bayonet except for the serial number on the hilt.

After the war the government turned to the centerfire cartridge — making percussion arms obsolete. By 1866 the army was already issuing the new 50/70 Springfield. At this time, i.e. June, 1866, the llth Ohio Cavalry located at Fort Leavenworth, Kansas had an assortment of arms consisting of three Merrill rifles, twenty-seven Spencer rifles, thirty-three Joslyn carbines and one hundred eighteen Spencer carbines.[17] When the llth Ohio was mustered out on July 14, 1866, they brought to a close the use of the Merrill rifle in Federal service.

The quantities of small arms acquired by the government during the war were so vast that they were compelled to continue disposing of these surplus goods right up to the turn of the century. On June 16, 1872, the New York Arsenal sold four hundred thirty Merrill rifles at prices ranging from fifteen cents each for two hundred eighty-five rifles to forty-five cents each for another one hundred forty-five. As late as June 20, 1892, two Merrill rifles were sold at the New York Arsenal for seventy-five cents each.[18]

The end of the war — and the era of the percussion breech-loader — brought the demise of the Merrill firm which ceased trading in 1869.

[1]U.S. Patent Office, U.S. Patent No. 20,954 of July 20, 1858.
[2]U.S. Patent Office, U.S. Patent No. 32,033 of April 9, 1861.
[3]Executive Document No. 99, 40th Congres, 2nd Session.
[4]NARG 156-994.
[5]Executive Document No. 99, 40th Congress, 2nd Session.
[6]L.D. Satterlee, *10 Old Gun Catalogs, Merrill Catalog:* Chicago; 1962, p. 22.
[7]Ibid, p. 23.
[8]NARG 156-111.
[9]NARG 156-108 & 111.
[10]NARG 156-110.
[11]Frederick H. Dyer, *A Compendium of the War of the Rebellion* Vol. II, Dayton, 1978, p. 1110 & 1111.
[12]Satterlee, op. cit., p. 24.
[13]Ibid, p. 28.
[14]Ibid, p. 26.
[15]Executive Document No. 99, 40th Congress, 2nd Session.
[16]Ibid.
[17]NARG 156-110.
[18]NARG 156-125.
[19]Executive Document No. 99, 40th Congress, 2nd Session.

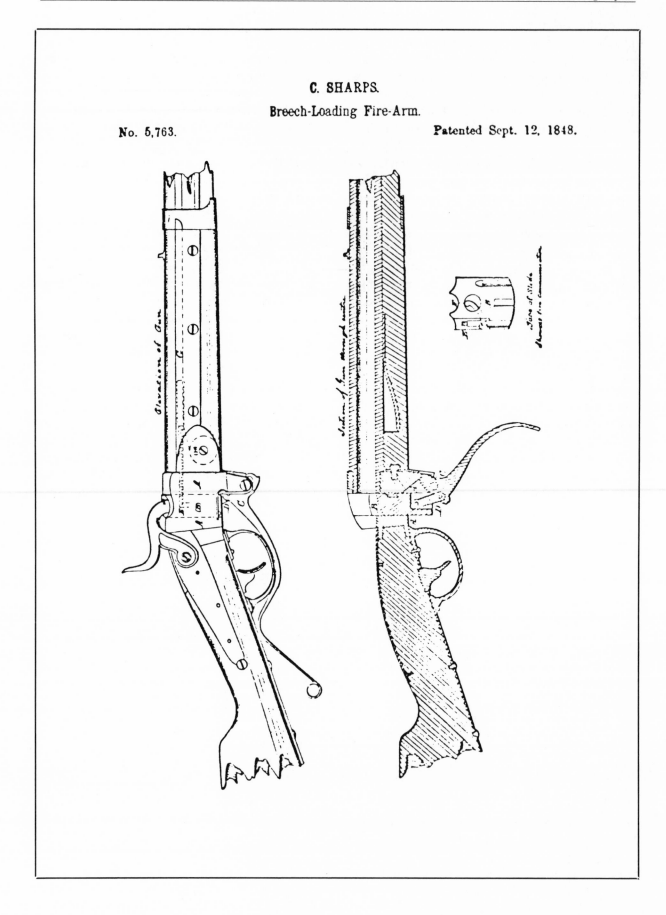

C. SHARPS.
Breech-Loading Fire-Arm.

No. 5,763.   Patented Sept. 12, 1848.

THE M1855 SHARPS NAVY RIFLE

By 1856, the Sharps Rifle Manufacturing Company was well established as an arms manufacturer of rifles and carbines. In the short four years since their incorporation at Hartford, Connecticut on October 8, 1851, they had already furnished arms to both the U.S. Army and Navy. In addition, a significant number of civilian sales had also been received.

In September of 1855, they entered into an agreement with the British Government to furnish six thousand Sharps breech-loading carbines equipped with Maynard tape primers. While the Sharps firm was responsible for the delivery of this British order the actual manufacturing was turned over to the well known, and technically advanced, firm of Robbins and Lawrence. At nearly the same time the U.S. Ordnance Department ordered four hundred carbines, also with Maynard tape primers, to be made at the Sharps plant.

The Maynard tape primer system had become the official ignition system for the U.S. Government at the direction of then Secretary of War Jefferson Davis in July of 1855 and reamined officially in use until 1861 at which time the Ordnance Office reverted to the use of the conventional percussion cap.

The Maynard tape priming system had been invented by Dr. Edward Maynard and patented by him on September 22, 1845 with U.S. Patent No. 4,208. Maynard's system eliminated the need to manually place a percussion cap on the nipple every time the weapon was ready for firing. Instead, the tape primer (which strongly resembled a roll of toy pistol caps) advanced by cocking the hammer, which placed the next primer in the roll over the nipple. Squeezing the trigger dropped the hammer on the primer causing the charge to be ignited.

In addition to the Maynard tape primer system, the Model 1855 Sharps Navy rifle was covered, as were all of the Sharps firearms, by Christian Sharps' original U. S. Patent No. 5763 dated September 12, 1848 for a sliding breech-pin and self-capping gun.

Christian Sharps actual patent claim read:

'What I claim as my invention, and desire to secure by Letters Patent, is —

1. The combination of the sliding breech with the barrel, the breech supporter, and the stock in such a manner that when the sliding breech is forced down the breech bore will be so exposed as to enable it to receive a cartridge on a line with the bore, and when the sliding breech is forced up it will shear off the rear end of the cartridge, so as to expose the powder to the fire communication, and will firmly and securely close the breech bore, substantially as herein set forth.

2. The combination of the cap nipple with the sliding breech, substantially in the manner and for the purpose herein set forth.'[1]

Early in 1856, John A. Dahlgren at the Washington Navy Yard wrote to the Sharps factory requesting that they send a carbine and rifle forward for testing and inquiring at what price would they furnish the U.S. Navy with two hundred of each.

On March 14, 1856, Dahlgren wrote John Palmer at the Sharps factory that the Navy would place an order for one hundred fifty Sharps rifles at $36 each. Dahlgren's letter to Palmer stated in part:

'Please furnish for the use of the Navy, 150 of the Sharps rifles according to sample sent by you to this office, including rod, brush, cone wrench, screwdriver, extra cone, cartridge stick, ball mould and with the following exceptions, viz.

The U.S. Navy nipple is to be substituted

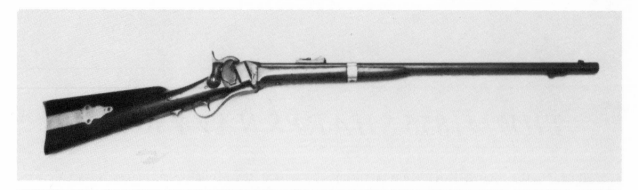

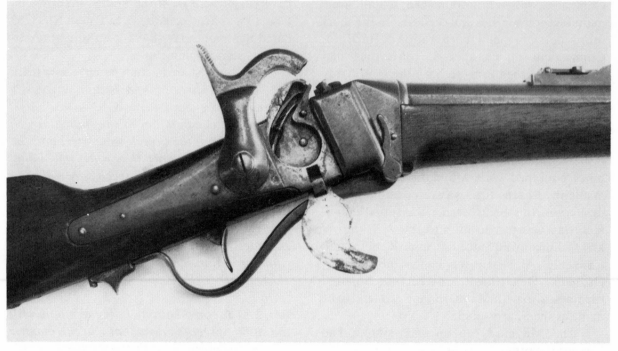

(above) Two hundred of these Model 1855 Sharps rifles were delivered to the U.S. Navy between September of 1856 and June 5, 1857. (below) Close-up of the lockplate of the 1855 Sharps rifle with the door of the Maynard Tape Primer open. The numerals stamped on the inside of the primer door are a patent royalty number.

— Authors' collection.

for your own.

The Maynard Primer is to be substituted for the Sharp Primer.

Please send 100 rounds of ammunition and 300 primers for rifle.

One hundred of these rifles are to be delivered within 20 days — 50 at New York and 50 at Norfolk.'[2]

In addition to the payment of $36 for the rifle and appendages the price for ammunition was set at $15 per one thousand rounds and primers at $1 per one thousand.

Five days later, Dahlgren again wrote Palmer stating that the Navy would give fifty days for delivery of the rifles, and that he did not

wish to place an order for any carbines at this time. Dahlgren goes on by saying that a *'ship leaving within 30 days for station infested with pirates and your arm might be called on to exhibit its capacity.'*[3] John Palmer made his official acceptance to the March 14 order on March 29.

In an April 24, 1856 letter from Dahlgren to Palmer, the Navy asked that fifty of the one hundred fifty Sharps rifles ordered on March 14 be furnished with the Rollin White's self-cocking device. This invention of Whites' — U.S. Patent No. 12,529, March 15, 1855 — was an attempt to automatically cock the hammer through the operation of the lever. Dahlgren's letter con-

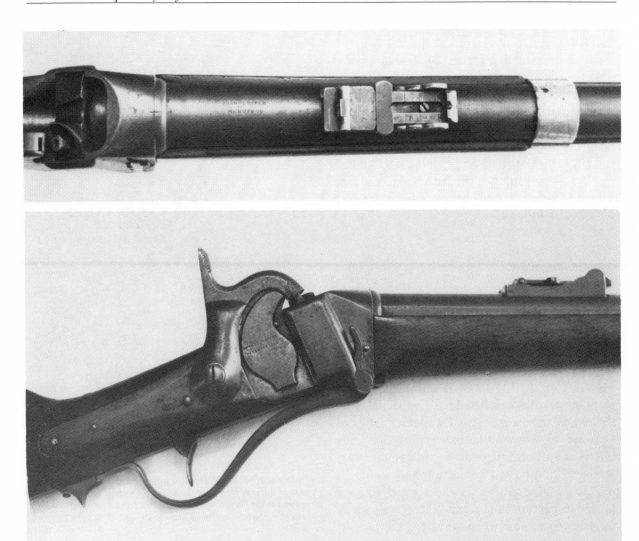

(above) The Sharps Model 1855 rifle seen from the top — illustrating the rear sight which is graduated to 800 yards. (below) The breech section and rear sight of the 1855 Sharps as seen from the side. Note the closed Maynard Tape Primer door stamped in two lines: **EDWARD MAYNARD/PATENTEE 1845.** This rifle is serial number 20,297.

     — Authors' collection

tinues by stating:

'The Merrimac leaves in a week for sea and it is highly desirable that some of the Sharps rifles should go with her.'[4]

During this period of time, April 1856, the Sharps factory had completed three hundred of the Army's order for four hundred carbines and the complete order was ready by May 15.

As of June 18, the Navy still had not received their Sharps and it was not until June 23 that Palmer was able to write Dahlgren at the Washington Naval Yards that the one hundred fifty rifles contracted for were nearly ready to be shipped.

Finally, on August 28, 1856, Palmer was able to state to Dahlgren that one hundred of these rifles had been sent forward to Washington and the remaining fifty with the White device would be sent in the course of a week. In addition, Sharps was willing to sell the Naval Department an additional fifty rifles. On September 3, Dahlgren passed this information of the sale of the additional fifty Sharps rifles to the Chief of Ordnance, Captain Ingraham. Getting the approval for the additional fifty rifles, Dahlgren contacted Palmer by letter on September 9 that he had the authority to accept them. He gave this order even though the March 14 order had still not arrived.

Shortly after the September 9 correspondence between the Navy and Palmer, the one hundred fifty rifles arrived at the Washington Navy Yard. On September 24, Dahlgren was able to write to Palmer and state that the first one hundred rifles had been inspected and were accepted and that payment would be sent. The fifty with the White self-cocking arrangement were then under examination. In addition, the last fifty rifles ordered on September 9 still had not been received as of the 24th. In accounting for payment on the one hundred rifles, they were itemized as follows:

100 Sharps Rifles with appendages	$3600.00
15 Packing boxes	37.50
50 Maynard Primer boxes	50.50
15 Cartridge boxes	232.50
Total Cost for 100 rifles	$3920.50[5]

Up to this point, the Sharps factory had been late on their orders but had received payment on all rifles which had been inspected. This trend was to change with Dahlgren's letter of October 17 when he had to report that only thirty-one of the fifty rifles ordered on September 9 had passed inspection and would be paid for. Eighteen of the nineteen which had not passed inspection had breech-plate screws which were found to be broken off just at the trigger-plate which they entered, plus the remaining one had a crack across the sliding breech-plate. Palmer asked for clarification for the reasons they were rejected and received this answer, *'it is the front vertical screw which cuts the stock immediately in rear of breech clean through to the trigger plate and right angle to the hammer screw.'*[6]

If this letter was not bad enough, Palmer received further bad news on October 24 when he was notified that only twelve of the fifty rifles with the White device had passed inspection and would be paid for at $36 each. Of the thirty-eight which did not pass inspection, twenty-six were found not to allow the chamber to open sufficiently to receive the charge and in many others the springs for the self-cocking arrangement were too weak. Therefore, in a span of a week, October 17-24, Palmer had received the bad news that only forty-three of the last one

Admiral John A. Dahlgren — long time chief of the Navy Ordnance Bureau. As a Captain, in 1856, he ordered the first Sharps rifles for the Navy and continued to exercise considerable influence over the choice Naval arms to the end of his colorful career.
— National Archives

hundred Sharps rifles would be paid for. With delays on the delivery of the British order and now having fifty-seven out of one hundred rifles rejected by the U.S. Navy, this created a real problem for John Palmer. The Navy did, however, sympathize with his problems and allowed the Sharps to be returned to the company and for them to make the necessary corrections so that they would meet the inspection requirements. On March 15, 1857, the nineteen rifles rejected on October 19 were returned and accepted and finally on June 5, 1857, the thirty-eight Sharps rifles with the White device were returned after removing the device and were now accepted and paid for at $36 each.[7]

Turning to the .52 caliber rifle itself we find that its overall length is forty-four and one-quarter inches with a weight of nine pounds. The case-hardened lockplate is fitted with the

NAVAL PROCUREMENT OF MODEL 1855 SHARPS RIFLES[8]

CONTRACTOR'S OR SELLER'S NAME	DATE OF PURCHASE	QUANTITY OR KIND OF STORES	PRICE	AMOUNT	DATE OF CONTRACT OR ORDER
Sharps Rifle Manufacturing Co.	9/24/56	100 Sharps Rifles & appendages	$36.00	$3,600.00	3/14/56
	10/17/56	31 Sharps Rifles & appendages	$36.00	$1,116.00	9/9/56
	10/24/56	12 Sharps Rifles with Whites' device	$36.00	$432.00	3/14/56
	3/15/57	19 Sharps Rifles	$36.00	$684.00	9/9/56
	6/5/57	38 Sharps Rifles	$36.00	$1,368.00	3/14/56
TOTAL		**200 Sharps Rifles**		**$7,200.00**	

Maynard tape-primer. The primer door is marked EDWARD MAYNARD/PATENTEE 1845. The lockplate is unmarked except for the fifty with the Rollin White device which will be marked ROLLIN WHITE'S/PATENT/1855. The forestock and buttstock are of black walnut. The buttplate, patchbox and barrel band are made of brass.

The twenty-eight and one-quarter inch round barrel is fitted for the bayonet lug on the bottom of the barrel for the sabre bayonet. The long range rear sight is graduated to eight hundred yeards. The barrel is marked SHARP'S RIFLE/MANUFG. CO/HARTFORD CONN. The tang will be marked SHARPS'/PATENT/

1848 with the serial number directly to the rear of this marking.

When the *U.S.S. Plymouth* sailed from Norfolk, Virginia on June 4, 1858, the M1855 Sharps rifles were aboard. With the war less than three years away, it is highly likely that these rifles were still in Naval service and saw action during the conflict. Ironically, success caused the demise of the Model 1855 Sharps on active service. The Navy was apparently pleased enough with the performance of this rifle to purchase larger numbers of the newer Model 1859 soon after the outbreak of the war — thereby forcing the replacement of the Model 1855 after a relatively short military career.

[1]U.S. Patent Office, U.S. Patent No. 5763 of September 12, 1848.
[2]NARG 74-145.
[3]Ibid.
[4]Ibid.
[5]Ibid.
[6]Ibid.
[7]Ibid.
[8]Ibid.

A Union Sergeant posing with his Sharps rifle. While the photo is not very clear it appears that this non-com is holding one of the double-set trigger military rifles of the type carried by Berdan's sharpshooters.
— Herb Peck Jr. collection

THE M1859 & M1863 SHARPS RIFLES

In 1858 the Sharps Rifle Manufacturing Company undertook making a number of major changes in the design of their carbines and, later on, their rifles. Richard S. Lawrence, who had left Robbins & Lawrence to become superintendent of the Sharps factory, had been working on improvements providing a better gas seal at the breech. Lawrence moved the entire breechlock section forward and placed it at right angles to the axis of the bore. He found that this arrangement worked better than the 'slant breech' design used up until this time. The adoption of this 'straight breech' constitutes the major difference between the older Sharps models and the New Models of 1859 and 1863.

While R. S. Lawrence's patent for his improved gas check method was not issued to him until December 20, 1859, it had been in use for about a year. In his December 20 Patent No. 26,501, Lawrence's claim read:

'What I claim as my invention and desire to secure by letters Patent is:

1. The combination of the detachable plate B between the barrel and the sliding breech, with the expanding ring cc, substantially as and for the purposes set forth.

2. In combination with the sliding breech and plate, the hollow nipple F, situated in the center of the gas chamber, and projecting forward nearly or quite to the face of the breech, substantially as and for the purpose herein set forth.'[1]

This patent was an improvement on the earlier H. Conant patent of April 1, 1856. Sharps breechblocks are found marked with both the 1856 and 1859 dates.

In addition to the gas check, two other major improvements are found on the new straight breech models. First was the change made to the rear sights. On February 15, 1859,

Lawrence was issued U.S. Patent No. 22,959 for improvements in adjustable sights for firearms. This patent claim read:

'What I claim as my invention, and desire to secure by letters Patent is:

The application of said hinge joint to the spring-base and elevator, constructed and arranged substantially as described.'[2]

The second change concerned an improved cut-off for the pellet priming system which had been invented by Christian Sharps before he left the Sharps Rifle Manufacturing Company in 1853. Sharps had been issued U.S. Patent No. 9,308 on October 5, 1852 for this system. To operate this primer system, a brass tube containing twenty-five copper pellet discs was inserted into the lockplate forward of the hammer. The hammer action threw the pellet forward where it was caught in mid air by the falling cock and crushed on the nipple. Lawrence's pellet cut-off system allowed the pellet-feed mechanism to be disengaged — the rifle to use the ordinary percussion cap instead of the pellet primers and the primers to be held in reserve. This patent, No. 23,590, was issued on April 12, 1859.

The advantage of being able to use either the primer or percussion cap can be shown in an incident which occurred at Chancellorsville on May 2, 1863. During the battle, a Berdan sharpshooter had his cap box shot away but with his Sharps rifle well supplied with pellet primers was able to continue. The sharpshooters did find that the percussion caps were more reliable than the primers which would frequently fail to explode the cartridge.

The first straight breech Sharps rifles were of the New Model 1859, usually found with thirty-inch barrels and an overall length of forty-seven and one-eighth inches. These rifles weigh eight pounds twelve ounces. While the majority of these rifles are equipped with a triangular bayonet but some have a lug fitted on the bottom of the barrel for the sabre type bayonet. There are also a small number of Sharps rifles with thirty-six inch barrels which are found in the serial number range of thirty-six thousand to thirty seven thousand.

The markings on the barrel are SHARPS RIFLE/MANUFG. CO./HARTFORD CONN. in three lines forward of the rear sight and NEW MODEL 1859 forward of the breech. The barrel is held to the forestock by three oval barrel bands. The rear sight graduated to seven hundred yards is the springbase type with a folding leaf and slide bar. The sight base is stamped R.S. LAWRENCE/PATENTED/FEB 15th, 1859.

The case-hardened back-action lock is marked to the rear of the hammer, C. SHARPS' PAT/OCT. 5th 1852 and above the hammer screw will be found R.S. LAWRENCE' PAT/APRIL 12th 1859. On the left side opposite the lock are the markings C. SHARPS' PAT./SEPT. 12th 1848 with the serial number located on the breech tang.

The buttstock is fitted for a case-hardened patchbox while the buttplate is unmarked. These New Model 1859 rifles are serial numbered between thirty six thousand and sixty thousand.

The Navy was first to place an order for the New Model 1859 Sharps rifle. In early September of 1859, they asked John C. Palmer at what price would the Sharps factory furnish the Navy with their rifle. In response to this inquiry, Palmer wrote on September 6 that the price would be $37.50 each. Finding this price acceptable, on September 9, 1859 the Navy entered into a contract with John Palmer for nine hundred Sharps .56 caliber rifles with sword bayonet and scabbard at the stated price of $37.50 each.[3] The sword bayonets were to be manufactured by Ames Manufacturing Company of Chicopee, Massachusetts. On this same date, the Navy also placed orders for five hundred Joslyn percussion rifles and one hundred Colt revolving rifles.

It would be over a year before the first delivery could be made. Finally on December 13, 1860, J.A. Dahlgren wrote Captain Buchanan, Chief of Naval Ordnance, at the Washing-

ton Navy Yard that he had inspected the first three hundred Sharps rifles. These rifles were of .56 caliber with a thirty inch barrel and fitted for the sabre bayonet. In his report to Captain Buchanan, Dahlgren states that the bullet used with these .56 caliber rifles weighed five hundred fifty grains and used seventy grains of powder.[4] While Dahlgren found the recoil strong, it was not excessive. Four days later on December 17 the second lot of three hundred thirty rifles was received at the ordnance yard in Washington. Two more deliveries were received in 1861 with the last lot of one hundred fifty rifles being received on April 13, 1861. In all, nine hundred thirty rifles were delivered on the September 9 contract, all being in .56 caliber, thirty inch barrel and fitted for the sabre bayonet.[5]

These rifles were quickly placed on board the *'Mississippi'* and *'Vincennes'* which were being outfitted for naval service. They also replaced the damaged Jenks carbines on the *'St. Lawrence'*. In early May of 1861, two hundred of these Sharps rifles were sent from New York to Boston while the Boston Naval Yard also received an additional eighty Sharps and fifty thousand .56 caliber cartridges from the Washington Navy Yard. During this period, seventy rifles were sent to Philadelphia from Washington. Even with these transfers of Sharps to the various navy yards, the Navy could not keep up with the demands for them. On May 20, Captain Harwood wrote to New York stating that he had no extra Sharps on hand. The only small arms available were smoothbore percussion muskets which the Navy Department had accepted from the Army. These arms would have to do until further breechloaders could be obtained.

To help supply this critical need for breechloaders, the Navy turned to John T. Mitchell of Washington, D.C. to furnish them with one thousand five hundred Sharps rifles. On June 4, 1861, a contract was entered into between Andrew A. Harwood, Chief of Naval Ordnance and John Mitchell. The contract stated in part:

'That the said John T. Mitchell hereby agrees to deliver at the Navy Yards at Boston-New York and Philadelphia 450 Sharps rifles on or before the 10th day of June present being 150 at each said yards, and Ten Hundred and Fifty of said Sharps rifles at said Navy Yards of Bos-

ton, Philadelphia and New York, that is to say 350 at each of said yards on or before the 25th day of June (present).'[6]

The price to be paid for Mitchell's order of Sharps rifles, which were in .52 caliber, was set at $43 each including appendages ie. brush, cone wrench screwdriver, extra cone, extra primer springs and one bullet mould for each five rifles.[7] The sabre bayonets were ordered from the Ames Sword Company of Chicopee, Massachusetts on June 5.

When the first one hundred fifty rifles were not delivered at the New York Navy Yard by June 10, Captain Harwood wrote to Mitchell on June 13 stating *'since this is an urgent and imperative demand for those arms, your immediate attention is called to this matter'.*[8] The next day Harwood directed the Boston Navy Yard to use their first delivery of one hundred fifty rifles to replace as fast as possible the Jenks carbines in all vessels being fitted out of Portsmouth for sea duty.

On August 9, 1861, Mitchell made deliveries of one thousand rifles to the New York Navy Yard in two lots of five hundred rifles each packed in chests holding ten rifles apiece. The price paid for each of these packing chests was set at $3. Six days later on August 15, the last five hundred rifles on the June 4 contract were received at the Boston Navy Yard. The total cost on this contract came to $64,950 which included the one thousand five hundred Sharps rifles and one hundred fifty arms chests.[9]

Having the Sharps rifles in both .52 and .56 caliber caused the Navy a great deal of headaches in supplying ammunition for them. In a September 1861 letter written from the Philadelphia Navy Yard to Washington, they complained that the one hundred Sharps rifles received at Philadelphia were of .52 caliber instead of the .56 caliber then presently in storage there.

In 1862 John Palmer was notified by the Navy that no additional carbines or rifles were needed. For the balance of the war the only transactions occurring between the Sharps factory and the Navy were for spare parts and ammunition.

During this same period, the Ordnance Department was also busy in the procurement of Sharps firearms. Their first open market purchase for the Sharps rifles came on June 11, 1861 when the Ordnance Office obtained one hundred nine rifles with sword bayonets from the New York firm of C.C. Bean. These rifles were purchased for the use of General Ben Butler's command at Baltimore. Later in the year, when additional sabre bayonets were needed for these rifles, the following request was made to the Sharps factory. General James Ripley wrote on October 14, 1861:

'SIR: Be pleased to send Colonel G. K. Warren, commanding Duryea's Zouaves, Federal Hill, Baltimore, care of Major Belger, quartermaster United States Army, 25 sword bayonets for Sharps rifles.'[10]

Colonel Warren's Duryea's Zouaves (5th New York Infantry) were sent their sabre bayonets the next day. Nearly two months later on December 7, an additional one hundred fifty sabre bayonets were delivered by the Sharps factory. All sabre bayonets were purchased at a cost of $4.50 each.

The only procurement of Sharps rifles made by the Ordnance Department in 1861 directly from the Sharps Rifle Manufacturing Company occurred on September 16 when one hundred rifles were purchased at a price of $42.50 each. While this was the only delivery by Sharps in 1861, the largest open market 1861 purchase occurred on August 15 when six hundred fifty-five rifles were received from the Union Defense Committee of New York. The price paid for these Sharps rifles ranged from $35 to $45 each.

The year 1861 also saw the formation of the most famous units to be issued the Sharps rifle. They were Berdan's 1st and 2nd U.S. Sharpshooters. To be accepted as a member of Berdan's sharpshooters, an individual firing at a target at two hundred yards had to place ten consecutive shots, the average distance not to exceed five inches from the center of the bull's-eye. Hiram Berdan had made his proposal to form such a regiment on June 13 and it was accepted by the government two days later. The majority of the 1st regiment of USSS was organized by September with the 2nd USSS formed by October.

The type of small arms to be issued to the

sharpshooters became a struggle between Ripley at the Ordnance Department and Berdan. Ripley was all in favor of issuing the muzzle-loading Springfield rifle musket while Colonel Berdan and his men were in favor of the breech-loading M1859 Sharps rifle. To press his case for the Sharps rifles, Colonel Berdan on October 22, 1861, wrote directly to Secretary of War Simon Cameron. The letter stated that a sample Sharps rifle which Berdan considered as the most suitable weapon to be placed in the hands of his men was being sent for the Secretary's inspection. The letter continues:

'Mr. J.C. Palmer Prest, of the Sharps Mang. Compy informs me that he can furnish say 3000 of these guns commencing to give us 100 a day after 20 days on receipt of the order and without any interference with the present Government order for carbines. We have about 200 heavy target rifles which is as many as I care to have of these heavy guns. We are exceedingly anxious to have these improved breechloaders with long bayonets. The price is $43 but this includes fly lock, double triggers & the long bayonet with sheath. The additional charge of 50 cts over the ordinary gun is certainly very reasonable for the extra work.'[11]

At the time the October 22 letter was sent the only Sharps rifle in the hands of the sharpshooters belonged to Private Truman Head of Co. 'C' 1st USSS, better known as 'California Joe'. He had purchased his rifle individually while at the Camp of Instruction in Washington, D.C. This Sharps rifle was fitted with the sabre bayonet and single set trigger.

Colonel Berdan eventually got his way and had the Sharps ordered for his men having to settle however for the angular bayonet in place of the sword bayonet. Ripley placed the order with Palmer for one thousand Sharps rifles with accoutrements for Berdan's Sharpshooters by telegram on January 27, 1862. Ten days later General Ripley placed a second order for an additional one thousand Sharps to be issued to the 2nd USSS. The order of January 27 reads:

'Send 1,000 Sharps rifles with accoutrements, and 100,000 cartridges, to Washington Arsenal for Berdan's sharpshooters. More by mail.

Send as soon as possible.[12]

Colonel Hiram Berdan — the well known Union officer who formed the 1st and 2nd United States Sharpshooters in the Fall of 1861. The Sharps military rifle with double-set triggers used by these units is still known as Berdan's Sharps.

— National Archives

That of February 6 reads:

'SIR: Be pleased to furnish this department with 1,000 Sharps rifles as soon as possible. These rifles should be made in the same manner and supplied with the same appendages and accoutrements as those lately ordered by this department for the use of a regiment of Berdan's Sharpshooters. I desire that you will also supply 100,000 cartridges suitable for these arms.'[13]

Not surprisingly, General Ripley became very upset when he learned that Colonel Berdan was corresponding directly with John Palmer regarding variations to the Sharps rifles, i.e. the addition of double set triggers. On March 12, Ripley warned Palmer that if the variations requested by Berdan caused a delay in delivery or higher costs then the responsibility must be borne directly by Palmer. Ripley's complaint appeared to have had no effect on the order

The breech section of one of the double-set trigger rifles used by the United States Sharpshooters. Rifles used by Berdan's regiments appear to have serial numbers between 54,400 and 57,600 of which this is number 54,580.   — Andrew Mowbray collection

since a month later the rifles started to leave the factory to be forwarded to Berdan's men. The price paid was set at $42.50 each, the same price being charged for the rifle with sabre bayonet. In addition, it also appears that probably all of the Sharps rifles made under the orders of January 27 and February 6 were manufactured with the double set triggers.

John Taylor, a U.S. sub-inspector, was sent to the Sharps factory by the Ordnance Department to inspect the rifles made under these contracts. Therefore, all Berdan Sharps rifles will have the inspector's cartouche (J.T.). These .52 caliber New Model 1859 pattern rifles have a thirty-inch barrel fitted for the angular bayonet as well as the previously mentioned double set triggers.

John Taylor wrote on April 23, 1862 that he had sent forward six hundred Sharps rifles to Fort Monroe, Virginia for Berdan. These rifles left the factory in lots of one hundred each on April 11, 14, 16, 19, 21 and 23. Shipments continued until May 24 when the last of the two thousand Berdan's Sharps were received. The rifles for the lst USSS were received at Fort Monroe while the Sharps for the 2nd USSS were delivered at the Washington Arsenal. Company 'F' lst USSS was the first to receive their Sharps rifles while at Yorktown, Virginia on May 8.[14] The remainder of the regiment would receive theirs shortly thereafter. It would not be until June 1 that the 2nd USSS was issued their Sharps while at Fredericksburg. Both regiments had been issued Colt revolving rifles at the start of the 1862 campaign which they now turned in.

The serial number ranges of these Berdan Sharps have posed a question which has been asked for years. A possible answer to this question may be found in the records of the New York Historical Society. Among these records are the personal papers of Lieutenant Colonel Casper Trepp of the lst U.S. Sharpshooters. During the majority of the 1862-1863 period until his death at Mine Run, Virginia on November 30, 1863, Lt. Col. Trepp was the acting field commander of the lst USSS. In Trepp's daily activities as commander of the regiment, his personal papers reveal the serial numbers of a number of Sharps rifles issued to or turned in by his men to the regimental armorer. The serial numbers of Sharps rifles listed by Trepp are No. 54858, 55085, 55820, 56371, 56974, 57131, 57266, 56386, 57428, 57471 and 57574. These serial numbers would seem to indicate that the serial number range for the Berdan's Sharps were No. 54400 to 57600.[15] In this range will also be found some carbines and a few single trigger rifles with inspectors of other than John Taylor.

While it is beyond the scope of this chapter to give the regiment history of Berdan's Sharpshooters, the following few instances will give a good indication of their deadly effectiveness with their Sharps rifles. The principal duties performed by Berdan's men were as advance skirmishers. Being well ahead of the main battle lines, the sharpshooters trained their rifle sights on Confederate officers and their artillery.

In a July 26, 1862 skirmish with the Confederates at Orange Court House, Virginia, the 2nd USSS inflicted thirty casualties on the enemy at a range of seven hundred yards. The range and number of casualties being substantiated by prisoners taken after the conclusion of the action.

During General John Pope's Second Manasses campaign of August 10 to September 2, 1862, the 2nd USSS fired 200,000 rounds of ammunition. In this active campaign, the 2nd started with six hundred to seven hundred men and came out with only one hundred twenty-nine answering roll call on September 2.

On the second day at Gettysburg, July 2, 1863, Major General Daniel Sickles, commander of the 3rd Army Corps, ordered Colonel Berdan to take one hundred of his sharpshooters (Cos. D, E, F & I) of 1st USSS and two hundred men from the 3rd Maine Infantry as support and do a reconnaissance of the extreme left of the Union line. In a hotly contested twenty minute action with Brigadier General Cadmus Wilcox's Brigade of A.P. Hill's Third Corps, Berdan's small force was able to establish the location and intent of Major General Longstreet's attack. In this action with Wilcox's Alabama Infantry, the sharpshooters used an average of ninety-five rounds of ammunition per man. In his official reports on the battle, Colonel Berdan stated that his sharpshooters numbered only four hundred fifty men but

expended 14,400 rounds of Sharps ammunition during the battle.[16]

The above skirmishes give a good indication of the great effectiveness of the Sharps rifles in the hands of Berdan's Sharpshooters. After Gettysburg, they saw action in numerous skirmishes and battlefields until finally disbanded as sharpshooters on February 20, 1865.

How many Sharps rifles did Berdan's Sharpshooters have at any one time? An Ordnance Department report dated October 24, 1862 reveals that the 1st USSS was issued by company the following Sharps rifles: Co. 'A' - 34, Co. 'B' - 73, Co. 'C' - 65, Co. 'D' - 16, Co. 'E' - 36, Co. 'F' - 73, Co. 'G' - 57, Co. 'H' - 38, Co. 'I' - 43, Co. 'K' - 34. 39 more rifles were in the hands of the regimental armorer.[17] This adds up to a total of five hundred eight rifles in the hands of the 1st USSS as of October 24. A later ordnance report of June 30, 1864 show the 1st USSS with one hundred forty seven Sharps while the 2nd USSS had only one hundred eighteen.[18]

What became of the surplus Sharps rifles not needed by Berdan? The answer is found in a letter written by Colonel Berdan on September 16, 1862 to Major Frank Earle, A.A.G. of Morell's Division of the 5th Corps. In it Berdan complains of his surplus Sharps rifles being given to other commands and his difficulty in getting them back. He states:

'After much trouble [I] succeeded in getting back 300 rifles from the Col. of a Mich. Regt. and 197 which I had turned in at Fortress Monroe. I have about 650 still out, which are in the hands of the Bucktails, and I must have them for the recruits and Companies which are coming into my Command under the recent Call. Fifty (50) recruits for my Regt. have just arrived and more are on the way. I shall have them all armed and Equipped here before they leave for the Regt.'[19]

The Bucktails — 13th Pennsylvania Reserves — 42nd Pennsylvania Volunteers Infantry were issued the Berdan Sharps on August 10, 1862. Colonel Berdan's letter of September 16 goes on to show the circumstances in which the Bucktails were given the Sharps rifles.

'Before marching from Harrison's Landing, I received orders to turn in all extra arms for transportation. I turned in about 100 that

Company 'F' of the 42nd Pennsylvania Infantry armed with Sharps rifles at least some of which were obtained under questionable circumstances from stores rightfully belonging to Colonel Berdan's 1st United States Sharpshooters. Eventually some of these rifles were returned to Berdan's command.   — Cliff Breidinger collection, U.S. Army Military History Institute

belonged to men then in hospitals. These guns were given to some Bucktails that had, as I am informed, just returned from Richmond, of course, without arms. On their arrival here their officers represented to Mr. Watson that their Regt. was partly armed with Sharps Rifles and that there were enough at the Arsenal to arm the entire Regt. and they would like to have the Regt. all armed with them. Mr. Watson not knowing but the first really belonged to the Bucktails or that those at the Arsenal belonged to me and had been promised to my recruits, gave the Bucktails enough to arm the whole Regt.'[20]

The Bucktails eventually turned back a number of their Sharps. This is evidenced by the fact that as of December 31, 1862, they had on hand only one hundred forty Sharps rifles and a number of Springfield rifle muskets. Subsequent ordnance reports for September 30, 1863 would show them with one hundred fifty-three Sharps and as of December 31, 1863 with one hundred seventy-six rifles.[21]

The rarest of the M1859 rifles is the thirty-six inch barrel rifle musket of which only about six hundred were manufactured. Their serial numbers will be found in the 36,000 to 37,000 range. It is known that the 8th and 11th Connecticut Volunteer Infantry regiments were issued these thirty six inch Sharps. The quarterly ordnance reports for December 31, 1862 disclose that the 8th Connecticut had been issued ninety-two Sharps rifles and the 11th Connecticut with seventy-eight.[22]

The Sharps rifles were generally well received by the troops to whom they were issued. One such regiment was the 14th Connecticut Infantry. In a letter written August 27, 1864, by Colonel Theodore G. Ellis, Commander of the 14th Connecticut to John Palmer, Colonel Ellis stated that his regiment had two companies armed with the Sharps rifle while the remainder were armed with the Springfield rifle musket. As of the date of this letter, Colonel Ellis stated that his men had their Sharps for two years and they worked as good as the day they were received while the Springfields were in less satisfactory condition. It was his opinion that the Sharps were the best breechloaders in the hands of the soldiers in the field.

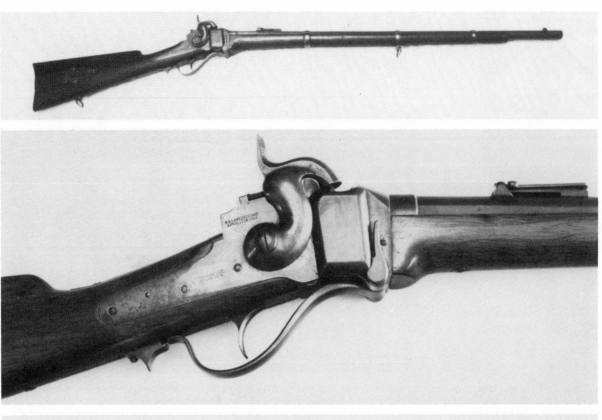

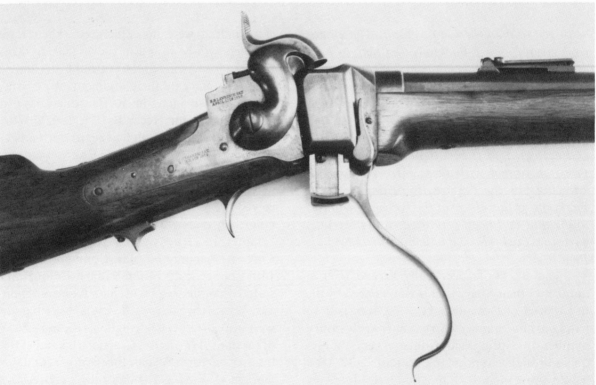

(top) Overall view of the Model 1863 Sharps rifle. In 1865, 6,150 of these rifles were delivered to the Ordnance Department. They are numbered approximately from C30,000 to C40,000 of which this is C37,856. (below) The breech section, open and closed, of the Sharps New Model 1859 rifle with the R.S. Lawrence patented rear sight. The first of these rifles had 36 inch barrels and carried a sabre bayonet. They are numbered in the 36,000 to 37,000 range of which this in number 36,660.   — Authors collection

He also had these interesting points to relate: that on the third day at Gettysburg, July 3, 1863, his men while attached to Brigadier General Alexander Hays' third Division of Major General Winfield Hancock's 2nd Army Corps were the first troops to break up Pickett's Charge. In this engagement, the 14th Connecticut ran out of Sharps .52 caliber ammunition for their rifles so they turned and used the .58 caliber Springfield ammunition without any apparent damage to their Sharps.

Presently (August 27, 1864) Colonel Ellis' command was located at Petersburg, Virginia. While in front of Petersburg, he states that his men were trying to pick off two of the enemy at a distance of one thousand one hundred yards with their Springfields. After several attempts, they gave up since the bullets failed to reach that distance. Two volunteers were then called to come forward with their Sharps rifles to attempt it, and with a couple of shots, both of the enemy were hit.[23]

The distance of one thousand one hundred yards quoted in Colonel Ellis's letter is open to question but it does show the great range and accuracy of the Sharps rifles. Colonel Ellis' 14th Connecticut saw further action at Petersburg and remained with the Army of the Potomac until May 21, 1865 when it was mustered out of federal service.

During the 1863 - 1864 period, the Ordnance Department had requested the officers in the field to comment on the breechloaders in their commands. While many responses were received on the Spencer, Henry and Colt revolving rifles, only one comment was recorded on the Sharps rifle and that report had been received from Captain George Ringland, Co. 'A' 11th Pennsylvania Cavalry. Captain Ringland considered that they *'carried well, did not get out of order easily, preferred a smaller caliber, and were not of much use for light cavalry service.'*[24] It would appear that the Captain's major objection was that the rifle was too cumbersome for cavalry use. This objection was a general view held by the cavalry.

All rifles discussed up to now have been of the New Model 1859, however, with the contract of December 1, 1864 for one hundred fifty Sharps rifles we see the first of the New Model

1863 rifle orders. The basic difference found between the M1859 and 1863 were the barrel markings - NEW MODEL 1863, improved cleanout screw in the breechblock and sight changes. The serial number range for these New Model 1863 rifles are from C30,000 to C40,000. Of the approximately seven thousand New Model 1863 rifles, only about one thousand were equipped with bayonet lug to take the sabre bayonet while the vast majority were fitted for the triangular bayonet.

The December 1, 1864 contract called for Sharps to deliver one hundred fifty .52 caliber rifles to the Ordnance Department and be paid $38 for each rifle which passed inspection. Later in December, Dyer wrote Palmer to request at what price they would be willing to supply the government with one thousand rifles. Palmer answered that the price would be $36 each. Finding this price too high, Dyer wrote Palmer on December 31 stating that $36 was unacceptable, but offering a contract at $33.50 each.

Haggling over the price continued on January 2, 1865 when Palmer turned down the government's latest offer and further stated that no more arms would be sold to the Ordnance Department at the current price since these contracts were causing Sharps to lose money. Dyer gave in to Palmer's complaints and placed an order for one thousand Sharps rifles with triangular bayonets at $36 each. This January 7, 1865 order read:

'SIR: You will please furnish to this department, and deliver to Colonel W.A. Thornton, inspector of contract arms, within fifty days from the date of this order, one thousand Sharp's breechloading rifles, with triangular bayonet and the necessary appendages, for which you will be paid at the rate of thirty-six dollars each for all that pass the usual inspection.'[25]

Palmer finding that he could not meet the fifty day delivery deadline wrote on February 20 requesting additional time which was granted by the ordnance office to extend delivery until March 18. Deliveries were made on March 21 while the previous order of December 1 was received on February 6.

The last wartime contract to be entered into between Palmer and Dyer occurred on March 7,

1865. It called for the delivery of five thousand Sharps rifles with triangular bayonets at a price of $33 each. General Dyer wrote Palmer on March 7, 1865:

'SIR: You will please furnish this department, and deliver to the inspector of contract arms, subject to the usual inspection, 5,000 Sharp's breech-loading rifles, with triangular bayonets and the usual appendages, for which thirty-three dollars ($33) each will be paid for all that pass the usual inspection and are received by the inspector. These rifles are to be adapted to use Sharp's primers. Deliveries are to be made at the rate of not less than 2,000 per month and are to commence on or before the fifteenth day of March, 1865.'[26]

The first rifle was not delivered until April 29. However, in May, two thousand twenty-eight rifles were received with the remaining two thousand nine hundred seventy-one rifles on the March 7 contract being received in June of 1865. This contract brought to a close the deliveries of Sharps arms purchased by the Ordnance Department. During the war years only the Spencers were obtained by the Government in larger quantities than the Sharps. For the period of 1859 when the New Model 1859 Sharps was introduced until the end of the Civil War approximately one hundred thousand straight breech model rifles and carbines were procured by the Army and the Navy.

The war years saw both Union and Confederate regiments armed at some time with Sharps rifles. The Confederate cavalry regiments partially armed with Sharps rifles were the 5th Virginia, 12th Tennessee and 13th Texas. Union regiments at least partially armed with Sharps rifles are given below.

INFANTRY REGIMENTS[27]

1st Connecticut	42nd Pennsylvania	2nd New Hampshire
2nd Connecticut	149th Pennsylvania	3rd New Hampshire
4th Connecticut	150th Pennsylvania	30th New Jersey
6th Connecticut	190th Pennsylvania	New York Independent Sharpshooters
7th Connecticut	11th Kentucky Mounted	2nd Indian Home Guard
8th Connecticut	15th Massachusetts	66th Illinois
11th Connecticut	Massachusetts Sharpshooters	113th Illinois
13th Connecticut	1st Minnesota	1st U.S. Sharpshooters
14th Connecticut	8th Minnesota	2nd U.S. Sharpshooters
20th Indiana	26th Missouri	3rd Michigan
11th Kentucky	2nd New York	5th Michigan
12th Kentucky	5th New York	16th Michigan
38th Pennsylvania	146th New York	37th U.S. Colored Infantry
	151st New York	4th Wisconsin

CAVALRY REGIMENTS[28]

1st Indiana	1st Illinois	1st Colorado
1st Iowa	13th Illinois	3rd Pennsylvania
3rd Iowa	15th Illinois	11th Pennsylvanis
5th Kansas	1st Kentucky	7th New York
6th Kansas	1st Louisiana (U.S.)	14th New York
7th Kansas	3rd Missouri	1st Maine
9th Kansas	4th Missouri	2nd Michigan
11th Kansas	7th Missouri	3rd Michigan
1st Minnesota	2nd U.S. Regulars	

NAVAL PROCUREMENT OF SHARPS RIFLES[35]

CONTRACTOR'S OR SELLER'S NAME	DATE OF PURCHASE	QUANTITY OR KIND OF STORES	PRICE	AMOUNT	DATE OF CONTRACT OR ORDER
Sharps Rifle Mfg. Co.	12/14/60	300 Sharps Rifles with appendages & sword bayonets	$37.50	$11,250.00	9/9/59
	12/19/60	330 Sharps Rifles with appendages & sword bayonets	$37.50	$12,375.00	9/9/59
	2/13/61	150 Sharps Rifles with appendages & sword bayonets	$37.50	$5,625.00	9/9/59
	4/13/61	150 Sharps Rifles with appendages & sword bayonets	$37.50	$5,625.00	9/9/59
John T. Mitchell	8/9/61	1,000 Sharps Rifles with appendages	$43.00	$43,000.00	6/4/61
	8/15/61	500 Sharps Rifles with appendages	$43.00	$21,500.00	6/4/61
TOTAL		**2,430 Sharps Rifles**		**$99,375.00**	

In 1866, while the regular infantry was turning in their muzzle loaders for the early trapdoor Springfields, the lst, 2nd, 3rd, 4th and 6th U.S. Veteran Volunteer Infantry regiments were armed with percussion Sharps rifles. These units were organized in early 1865 for duty in Washington D.C. and the Shenandoah Valley.

In the following year, 1867, the 10th U.S. Cavalry, while officially armed with Spencer carbines and M1860 Colt revolvers, still held twenty-four Sharps rifles in regimental storage.[29]

As of December 1, 1866, the Navy still held in inventory one thousand five hundred thirty .52 caliber rifles and eight hundred twenty-one .56 caliber rifles. (see below)

SHARPS RIFLES (12/1/66)[30]

Location	.52 Cal.	.56 Cal
Portsmouth, N.H.	73	72
Boston	112	
New York	653	77
Philadelphia	65	595
Washington	4	10
Norfolk	129	3
Jefferson Barracks	145	
Pensacola, Florida	341	44
Mare Island, Calif.	8	20
Total	**1,530**	**821**

The 1868 quarterly reports of target practice with small arms about the Naval vessels reveals the Sharps rifles were in use by the marine guards aboard the *USS Ticonderoga, USS Decotah* and the Steamer *Huron.*[31]

The close of the Civil War also saw the end of the percussion ignition era. The post war years would see the advancement of the 50/70 centerfire cartridge in use by the U.S. Army. At this period in time, the Government had in their stockpile nearly fifty thousand Sharps carbines and rifles. Of this amount, thirty five thousand were of the straight breech Models 1859 and 1863 with the remaining fifteen thousand of the earlier slant breech models. The slant breech models were not easily converted to centerfire and therefore were found to be obsolete. The straight breech models were, however, able to be converted to centerfire; and, therefore, to make these Sharps of more use, the government entered into the November 2, 1867 contract to alter the percussion Sharps to 50/70 centerfire. The price set for this conversion was $4.50 each.

Between February 25, 1868 and October 6, 1868, thirty one thousand ninety-eight conversion carbines were delivered. The rifles which were set aside early in this contract were converted to 50/70 centerfire and delivered at a rate of four hundred fifty rifles on July 19, 1869, two hundred fifty rifles on August 14 and three hundred eighty-six rifles on October 6. This made a total of one thousand eighty-six rifles converted to 50/70 by the Sharps Rifle Manufacturing Company.[32]

In addition to converting the Sharps rifles, others were sold outright by the Government on the open market at prices ranging from $1.55 to $7 each. For example, in 1876 the St. Louis Ordnance Department Arsenal sold one hundred thirteen Sharps rifles and as late as April 26, 1890 an additional twenty rifles were being sold at the Rock Island Arsenal for $4.50 each.[33] In 1865 discharged soldiers took three thousand four hundred fifty-four Sharps rifles home with them at a cost of $8 each.[34] After the general decline in business in the immediate post war years, the 1870's saw a general upswing in Sharps general business activity with the M1874 sporting and buffalo rifles. The firm was reorganized as the Sharps Rifle Company in 1874 and two years later move from Hartford to Bridgeport, Connecticut. Due to a number of financial problems, the firm closed its doors for good in October of 1881.

ARMY PROCUREMENT OF SHARPS RIFLES[36]

CONTRACTOR'S OR SELLER'S NAME	DATE OF PURCHASE	QUANTITY OR KIND OF STORES	PRICE	AMOUNT	DATE OF CONTRACT OR ORDER
C.C. Bean	6/11/61	109 Long Range Rifles with bayonets	$45.25	$4,932.25	6/9/61
	3/10/62	288 Sharps Rifles with bayonets	$40.25	$11,592.00	6/9/61
Tiffany & Co.	9/12/61	5 Sharps Rifles & implements	$34.00	$170.00	Purchase
J.M. Chivington	10/1/61	8 Sharps Rifles	$20.00	$160.00	Purchase
Union Defense Committee of New York	8/7/61	8 Sharps Rifles with bayonets	$35.00	$280.00	Purchase
	8/7/61	1 Sharps Rifle with bayonet	$35.00	$35.00	Purchase
	8/7/61	4 Sharps Rifles with bayonets	$35.00	$140.00	Purchase
	8/15/61	222 Sharps Rifles with bayonets	$45.00	$9,990.00	Purchase
	8/15/61	222 Sharps Rifles with bayonets	$35.00	$7,770.00	Purchase
	8/15/61	211 Sharps Rifles with bayonets	$40.00	$8,440.00	Purchase
Schuyler, Hartley & Graham	9/19/63	1 Sharps Rifle		$43.00	Purchase
	9/19/63	1 Sharps Rifle		$45.00	Purchase
Sharps Rifle Mfg. Co.	9/16/61	100 Army Rifles — Sabre bayonets	$42.50	$4,250.00	Purchase
	4/21/62	500 Sharps Rifles and appendages	$42.50	$21,250.00	1/27/62
	5/2/62	500 Sharps Rifles and appendages	$42.50	$21,250.00	1/27/62

CONTRACTOR'S OR SELLER'S NAME	DATE OF PURCHASE	QUANTITY OR KIND OF STORES	PRICE	AMOUNT	DATE OF CONTRACT OR ORDER
Sharps Rifle Mfg. Co. (cont.)	5/14/62	500 Sharps Rifles and appendages	$42.50	$21,250.00	2/6/62
	5/24/62	500 Sharps Rifles and appendages	$42.50	$21,250.00	2/6/62
	3/11/63	20 Sharps Rifles — Sabre bayonets	$42.50	$850.00	Purchase
	2/6/65	150 Sharps Rifles	$38.00	5,700.00	12/1/64
	3/21/65	1,000 Sharps Rifles with bayonets	$36.00	$36,000.00	1/7/65
	4/29/65	1 Sharps Rifle		$33.00	3/7/65
	5/11/65	1,028 Sharps Rifles with bayonets	$33.00	$33,924.00	3/7/65
	5/27/65	1,000 Sharps Rifles with bayonets	$33.00	$33,000.00	3/7/65
	6/10/65	1,000 Sharps Rifles with bayonets	$33.00	$33,000.00	3/7/65
	6/22/65	1,000 Sharps Rifles with bayonets	$33.00	$33,000.00	3/7/65
	6/30/65	971 Sharps Rifles with bayonets	$33.00	$32,043.00	3/7/65
	TOTAL	**9,350 Sharps Rifles**			

[1]U.S. Patent Office, U.S. Patent No. 26,501 of December 20, 1859.
[2]Ibid, U.S. Patent No. 22,959 of February 15, 1859. [3]NARG 74-157.
[4]NARG 74-145.
[5]NARG 74-158.
[6]NARG 74-165.
[7]NARG 74-165.
[8]NARG 74-6.
[9]NARG 74-157.
[10]Executive Document No. 99, 40th Congress 2nd Session.
[11]Wiley Sword, The Berdan Sharps Rifle, *Man at Arms,* July/August 1980, p. 41.
[12]Executive Document No. 99, 40th Congress, 2nd Session.
[13]Ibid.
[14]G.G. Bendict, *Vermont in the Civil War,* 2 vols. Burlington: 1888, p. 735.
[15]Wiley Sword, op. cit., p. 42
[16]Captain C.A. Stevens, *Berdan's U.S. Sharpshooters in the Army of the Potomac,* Dayton: 1972, p. 343.
[17]NARG 156-108.
[18]NARG 156-111.
[19]NARG 94.
[20]Ibid.
[21]NARG 156-111.
[22]Ibid.
[23]NARG 156-201.
[24]NARG 156-215.
[25]Executive Document No. 99, 40th Congress, 2nd Session.
[26]Ibid.
[27]NARG 156-111 and Frederick P. Todd, *American Military Equipage 1851-1872,* Volume II State Forces, Chatham Squire Press, 1983.
[28]NARG 156-110.
[29]Ibid.
[30]Executive Document No. 16-2, 39th Congress (December 31, 1866).
[31]NARG 74-101.
[33]Frank Sellers, *Sharps Firearms.* North Hollywood: 1978, p. 180.
[33]NARG 156-125.
[34]Francis A. Lord, *They Fought For The Union,* Harrisburg, 1960, p. 166 and 277.
[35]NARG 74-157.
[36]Executive Document No. 99, 40th Congress, 2nd Session.

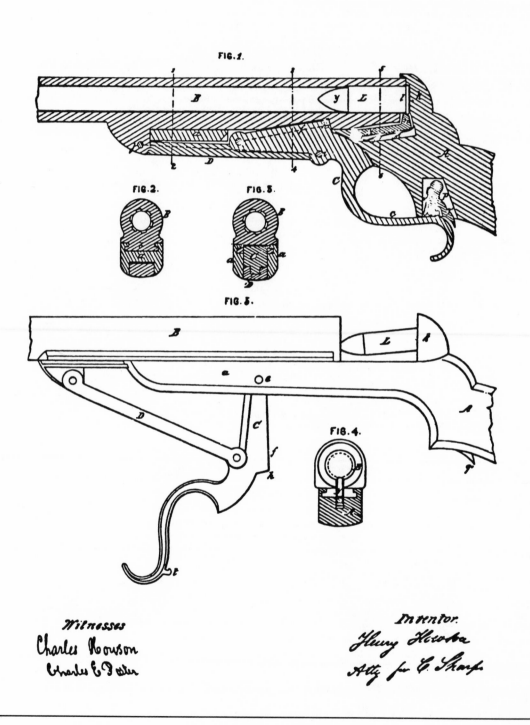

C. SHARP.
BREECH LOADING FIRE ARM.

No. 32,790.   Patented July 9, 1861.

FIG. 1.

FIG. 2.   FIG. 3.

FIG. 5.

FIG. 4.

Witnesses
Charles Rowson
Charles E. Potter

Inventor.
Henry Hoover
Atty. for C. Sharp

THE SHARPS & HANKINS NAVY RIFLE

In November of 1851, Christian Sharps traveled to the Robbins & Lawrence factory in Windsor, Vermont on behalf of the Sharps Rifle Manufacturing Company, to help place his Sharps firearms in mass production. In charge of the Robbins & Lawrence firm was Richard S. Lawrence. From the outset there was a mutual dislike between Sharps and Lawrence over the design changes which were necessary to get the Sharps firearms into production.

This dislike came to a head in October of 1852 when the Sharps company, which actually employed the inventor as a technical advisor, decided not to renew his contract. This did not seem to disturb Sharps since he still received a royalty of one dollar for every gun manufactured plus twenty-five cents for each lock made.[1]

A final agreement between Christian Sharps and the Sharps factory was made on April 10, 1854 for the royalties previously mentioned plus $4,000 and four hundred Model 1852 Sharps carbines.[2]

Sharps received the last two hundred carbines from this agreement on June 13th and promptly left for Philadelphia. Only two years earlier, on March 7, 1852, Christian Sharps had married Sara Elizabeth Chadwick in Philadelphia. They took up residence at 486 Green Street; and Sharps established his small shop at 336 Franklin Street.

Needing capital to expand his operation, Sharps formed a partnership with Ira B. Eddy, and in 1857, the firm was known as Eddy, Sharps & Company. Nathan H. Bolles also became a partner and in 1858, the firm's name was again changed to C. Sharps & Company which it remained until 1863 when it was changed to Sharps & Hankins.

From 1856 to 1864, the Sharps factory was located at the west side of 30th Street in West Philadelphia at the Wire Bridge. The four story brick building measured 140 feet by 40 feet. The factory's first floor consisted of the heavy forging operations, the second floor for barrel making, third floor for tool making, and the fourth floor for the manufacture of small parts and assembling operations.

In 1860, William C. Hankins, a woodmaker by trade, joined the firm as superintendent of the rifle works. He brought additional capital to the business which was greatly needed for further operations. In 1861, both Ira Eddy and Nathan Bolles left the firm. The following year Willian Hankins became a full partner, but it was not until 1863 that the firm's name was changed to Sharps & Hankins.[3]

The Sharps & Hankins Navy rifles are covered by three of Christian Sharps' patents. In U.S. Patent No. 32,790 of July 9, 1861, Sharps states in part: *'My invention relates to an improvement in breechloading firearms in which a barrel or barrels arranged to slide to and fro on the stock are used; and my improvement consists in a device, described hereinafter, for locking and releasing the lever which operates the barrel.'*[4]

The portion of this patent covering the sliding of the barrel was rejected by the Patent Office as having been anticipated by his own patent No. 22,752 of January 25, 1859. This claim was allowed, however, on Sharps patent No. 2,481 reissued on February 24, 1867. U.S. Patent No. 32,899 dated July 23, 1861 covered the rear sight used on the Sharps & Hankins while the safety mechanism was patented on October 22, 1861 with U.S. Patent No. 33,546.

The Sharps & Hankins firearms have a number of inital firsts for military arms which would include:

a) A separate firing pin within the receiver.

b) Hammer safety mechanism — this kept the hammer face from contacting the firing pin.

c) Extractor system — a spring loaded catch in the frame extracts the cartridge and also prohibits the forward movement of the cartridge case when the breech is open.

Sharps wasted little time after the outbreak of the war to have his rifle tested by the Navy Department On July 20, 1861, Lieutenant Wainwright test fired a Sharps & Hankins rifle five hundred times with fifteen failures caused by faulty rimfire ammunition. The defective ammunition was made of brass and it was the head of the cartridge which burst in firing. The features of the rifle tested were:

Diameter of the Bore	.5635 inches
Length of Rifle	47.28 inches
Length of Barrel	32.80 inches
Diameter of Ball	.56 inches
Length of Ball	.91 inches[5]

Nine days later, on July 29, 1861, the Navy contracted with Christian Sharps for five hundred of these rifles with sabre bayonets at $36 each. The first lot of one hundred rifles were to be delivered one week after January 29, 1862. The remaining rifles were to be received at a rate of one hundred each succeeding week.[6] Given these delivery dates, the first lot was due on February 5 and all were to be received by March 5. The July 29 contract also called for 50,000 metal cased cartridges adopted for the rifle at a cost of $19 per thousand.

Sharps did not make his scheduled deliveries, and on April 16 the Navy wrote Christian Sharps that he should send his first rifles to the New York Navy Yard. The first lot of 150 Sharps & Hankins were received and paid for on April 28. On May 5 William Temple, the assistant inspector of ordnance at the New York Navy Yard, was directed by Andrew Harwood, Chief of Naval Ordnance, to notify Sharps & Hankins that they had to replace one rifle received with a broken stock and ammunition found to be defective. They were also to send the spare parts needed for these rifles.[7] The second delivery of 150 rifles was sent to the Boston Navy Yard on May 27 and paid for on July 5 at a cost to the Navy of $5,892.14.[8]

The next installment on this contract was made on June 28, 1862 when one hundred rifles were delivered, this time at the Washington Navy Yard. The invoices for this lot show that the price was set at:

100 rifles at $36 each	$3,600.00
10M cartridges @ $19	$190.00
Extra parts for rifles	26.77
Total cost of Inventory Goods	$3,816.77[9]

(left and above) The 500 Sharps & Hankins rifles ordered by the United States Navy on July 29, 1861 were delivered between April 28 and September 22, 1862. (left) A close-up of the breech section of a Sharps & Hankins M1861 rifle — No. 295. Note the Sharps tangent type rear sight. (above) The Sharps & Hankins shown with the action open. Note how the entire barrel and forend slides forward on the grooved frame. Since this is an 'Old Model' the firing pin is mounted in the face of the hammer.   — Authors collection

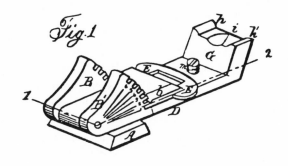

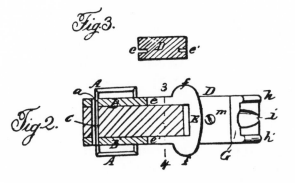

The drawing attached to the patent for Sharps' special rear sight — as used on the Sharps & Hankins rifle. It was quite commen for inventors of Sharps' talent to patent not only their basic arms but also every possible variation and accessory for them. Before the Civil War this was probably necessary since there was very little in the way of proprietary components available. After the war, and in light of the quantum leap made by all kinds of industrial/machine production as a result of the war's demands, this practice started to die out. Today it is almost invariably cheaper and better to purchase such components from specialist suppliers — something that did not exist in 1861.

Upon receipt of these last hundred rifles, Lieutenant Commander W.W. Green at the Washington Navy Yard had them tested. This test firing occurred on August 30, 1862. The Sharps & Hankins rifles used during these tests were serial numbered 565, 554, 547 and 568. After the tests were completed, Green submitted this conclusion, *'I respectfully report the rifles as fit for service.'*[10]

The final delivery on the July 29 contract was received at the Washington Navy Yard in September of 1862 when 100 rifles and 10,000 cartridges were received and paid for at a cost of $3,225.00.[11] It appears that no bayonets were received with this delivery.

On August 6, 1862 John Dahlgren requested that Sharps & Hankins deliver 250 carbines as soon as possible to the Philadelphia Navy Yard. The delivery site was later changed to New York. In November these carbines were sent to New York and also to Boston. Captain Channcey was sent to inspect these carbines. He found them to be defective and therefore rejected the entire lot.

In a letter dated December 8, 1862 from Sharps & Hankins to the Navy, Sharps made the requested that the last five hundred guns delivered to the Navy be returned to them so that they could alter them to use the Spencer cartridge (.56-.56).[12] It is apparent from this letter that Sharps was unaware his arms had been rejected.

The official notice of their rejection was sent on December 16 when Dahlgren's letter stated in part: *'These guns have been examined and rejected by the inspecting officer. They are therefore not received and are at the disposal of the maker.'*[13]

Due to the defects found in the carbines, Lieutenant Mitchell of the Washington Navy Yard was directed on December 13 to reinspect the 100 Sharps & Hankins rifles delivered there on June 28. No rifles were to be issued until the inspection was completed. Finding these rifles satisfactory for use, Dahlgren sent the following letter, dated December 24, to Sharps:

SIR: — In addition to previous orders the Bureau wishes you to send to the Ordnance Yard here, Twenty thousand (20,000) ball cartridges for the Sharps & Hankins rifles.[14]

The Sharps & Hankins rifles were used by the Navy to arm the Marine guards aboard ship. They were also put to use on the gun boats operating on the Mississippi River. In 1863, 60 of these rifles were sent to St. Louis to be used on these boats.[15]

While the records indicate that only five hundred Sharps & Hankins rifles were purchased by the Federal Government, many more carbines were obtained from Sharps & Hankins as shown in the following chart:

Procurement	Branch of Service	
By Year	Army	Navy
1862	250	250
1863	1,201	1,500
1864	—	4,380
1865	17	200
1867	—	6
	1,468	**6,336**

The Sharps & Hankins rifles were still in active service after the war as is shown by the inventory listed in the various naval yards as of December 1, 1866 when 214 rifles were located at the Washington Navy Yard. In addition, 3,004 Sharps & Hankins carbines were on hand.[16] In a report dated June 20, 1868 Lt. Commander Stuyvesant of the USS Wateree, gave

the following test firing results by the Marine Guard. The Sharps & Hankins rifles were fired at a distance of one hundred yards with these results:

Number of shots fired	339
Number of hits	85
Number of hits within six inches of bull's eye	13

Stuyvesant concluded his report with this statement: *'The Sharps & Hankins rifle is easily comprehended by the men and seems well adopted to the wants of the service*'[17]

The rimfire cartridges used in the Sharps & Hankins rifles had a bullet diameter of 0.555 inches and weighed 465 grains. The powder charge consisted of 55 grains and the length of case 1.16 inches with an overall length of 1.76 inches.

The Sharps & Hankins consisted of the 'Old Model' (1861) and the improved New Model (1862). This 'old' and 'new' model terminology was employed by the factory. Only about 750 of the 'Old Model' arms were manufactured. The highest known serial number carbine #736.

The basic difference between the Old Model and the improved New Model was the design of the hammer and firing pin. The Old Model had the firing pin in the hammer while the New Model had a floating firing pin in the rear of the receiver. It also had a stringer mainspring and added an oil hole to the extractor well.

The following description is of the Sharps & Hankins 'Old Model' (1861) since the Navy rifles were of this type. The rifle is .52 caliber rimfire using the (52-56) Sharps & Hankins cartridge. The overall length is 47 5/8 inches and it weighs 8 pounds 8 ounces. The black walnut stock is of two piece construction. The 32 3/4 inch barrel will be found blued or brown. It has an iron front sight and rear-sight of the Sharps base tangent type, graduated to eight hundred yards with the base notched at one hundred yard intervals. A bayonet lug will be found under the barrel for attaching the saber bayonet. The barrel is held to the forestock by three solid oval barrel bands.

The receiver is marked on the right side: SHARPS/&/HANKINS/PHILADA and on

NAVY PROCUREMENT OF SHARPS & HANKINS RIFLES[18]

CONTRACTOR'S OR SELLER'S NAME	DATE OF PURCHASE	QUANTITY OR KIND OF STORES	PRICE	AMOUNT	DATE OF PAYMENT
Sharps & Hankins Philadelphia, PA	4/28/62	150 Rifles w/Bayonets	$36.00	$5,783.25	4/28/62
	5/27/62	150 Rifles w/Bayonets	$36.00	$5,892.14	7/5/62
	6/28/62	100 Rifles w/Bayonets	$36.00	$3,816.77	11/25/62
	9/22/62	100 Rifles		$3,225.00	9/22/62
TOTAL		**500 rifles**		**$18,717.16**	

the left side: SHARPS/PATENT/1859. The serial number is on the upper tang and all major parts. The receiver, hamer, lever and tang are casehardened. The butt plate is made of brass.

The saber bayonet used with this rifle is twenty-five inches long and has a 20 1/4 inch blade marked COLLINS & CO. and dated 1861. The bayonets were serial numbered with the rifles.

To operate the Sharps & Hankins, the release is tripped on the operating lever catch which allows the lever to be moved down and forward. This slides the barrel forward along the mortised channels within the breech-frame and exposes the chamber for insertion of the rimfire cartridge.

Operations at the Sharps & Hankins factory ceased in 1867 and all guns were sold by early 1868. In late 1867, William Hankins left the firm and the name was changed to C. Sharps & Co. In 1867, Christian Sharps left Philadelphia and moved his residence to Vernon, Connecticut, where he lived until his death, from tuberculosis, on March 12, 1874. He left his wife, Sarah; a daughter, Satella; and a son, Leon Stewart Sharps. His estate was valued at $341.25.

[1]Frank Sellers, *Sharps Firearms,* North Hollywood: 1978, p. 103.
[2]Ibid.
[3]John D McAulay, *Carbines of the Civil War 1861-1865,* Union City: 1981, p. 95.
[4]U.S. Patent Office, U.S. Patent No 32,790 of July 9, 1861
[5]J. Richard Salzer, *The Sharps & Hankins Carbine,* The Gun Report, January 1863, p. 8.
[6]NARG 74-157
[7]NARG 74-6
[8]NARG 74-5
[9]NARG 74-158
[10]NARG 74-145
[11]NARG 74-6
[12]NARG 74-22
[13]NARG 74-5
[14]Ibid.
[15]NARG 74-3
[16]H.R. Executive Document No. 16-2, 38th Congress (Dec. 31, 1866)
[17]NARG 74-101
[18]NARG 74-5, 6, 158

A Union Cavalry Sergeant with his Spencer rifle, saber and what appears to be a Model 1860 Colt revolver. Note that he has removed the revolver from its holster — which he is still wearing — and stuck it in his belt where it can be seen.   Herb Peck Jr., collection

THE M1860 SPENCER RIFLE

The first truly successful repeating rifle to use a metallic cartridge was the Spencer. This firearm, with its seven shot repeating capacity, was one of the contributing factors in turning the Civil War in favor of the North.

The inventor, Christopher Miner Spencer, was born in South Manchester, Connecticut on June 20, 1833. At the age of fourteen, he went to work first for the Cheney Silk Mills and later for Samuel Loomis. By 1853 he was living in Rochester, New York working at repairing locomotives. In the next five years, Spencer worked for both N.P. Ames and then for Samuel Colt at the Colt Armory. In 1858 he returned to his original place of employment, the Cheney Brothers Silk Mills.

During this period of time, ie. 1858, Spencer conceived the idea for a repeating rifle, but it was not until 1859 that he successfully completed his basic design. In 1859 and 1860, Spencer and Luke Wheelock made at least twenty-eight Spencer carbines and rifles in .36 and .44 caliber using the facilities of the Cheney Brothers plant in Hartford, Connecticut.

Christopher Spencer received his original patent, No. 27,393, for his rifle design on March 6, 1860. In part, the patent reads:

'My invention consists in an improved mode of locking the movable breech of a breech-loading fire-arm, whereby it is easily opened and closed, and very firmly secured in place during the explosion of the charge.

It also consists in certain contrivances for operating in combination with the movable breech for the purpose of withdrawing the cases of the exploded cartridges from the chamber of the barrel and for conducting new cartridges thereinto from a magazine in the stock.'[1]

Two years later on July 29, 1862, Spencer received U.S. Patent No. 36,062 for an improved cartridge-retractor for breech-loading firearms. He states in the patent papers:

'This invention relates to breech-loading firearms in which are used metallic cartridges, whose cases, after having been discharged, require to be withdrawn from the chamber of the barrel in a rearward direction, more especially to those arms having a rolling breech substantially such as is described in Letters Patent No. 27,393, obtained by me in the year 1860, and loading from a magazine. It consists in an improvement in the means of withdrawing the discharged cartridge-cases from the barrel.'[2]

What I claim as my invention, and desire to secure by Letters Patent, is:

The arrangement of the hinged lever G with the breech-pieces B C, frame A, and tongue m, in the manner herein shown and described.'[3]

To operate the Spencer rifle, the operating lever is first lowered. This motion ejects the previously fired cartridge and brings the next cartridge into position to be fed into the receiver with the closing of the breech. The hammer is then manually cocked and the rifle is ready for firing. The tubular magazine for feeding the rimfire cartridge to the receiver is located in the buttstock. This tubular magazine holds seven rimfire cartridges and works with a coil spring.

The No. 56 rimfire cartridge (Spencer 56-56) used in the Civil War Spencer rifle has a bullet diameter of .54 and weighs four hundred thirty-three grains. The cartridge contains a powder charge of forty-five grains and has an overall length of 1.67 inches.

The first Spencer rifle 'No. 56 caliber' was made by Christopher Spencer between May 6-30, 1861, at a total cost of $293.67. To interest the government in this rifle, he sought the help of his employers, Charles and Frank Cheney. The Cheney's were neighbors and personal

C. M. SPENCER.

Magazine Gun.

No. 27,393.   Patented Mar. 6, 1860.

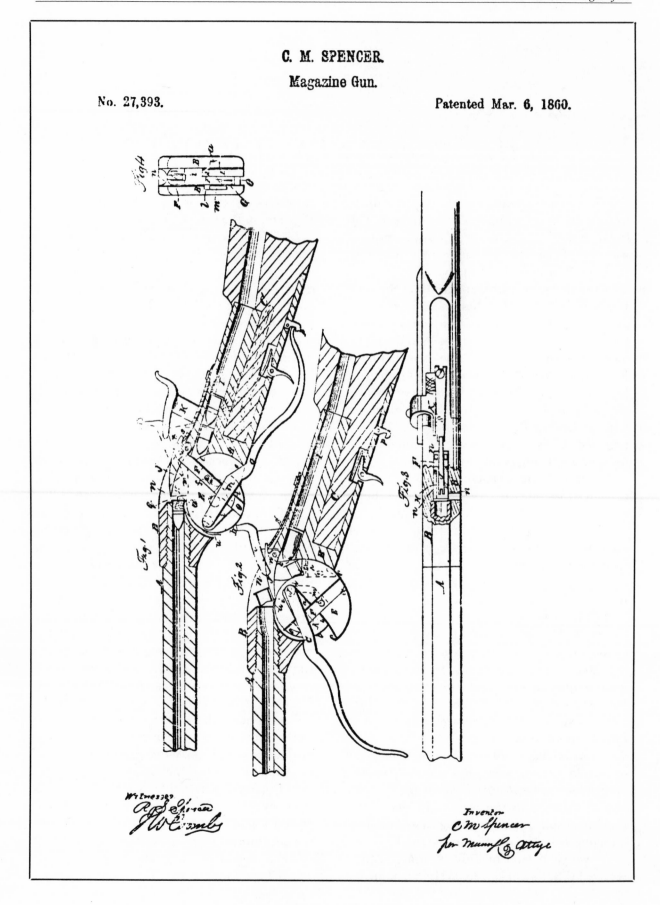

friends of Secretary of the Navy Gideon Welles and persuaded him to secure a Navy test of the rifle. It was field tested on June 8, 1861 by John A. Dahlgren who had this to say about the Spencer:

'An arm was presented here merely for examination which operates so well that I am induced to bring it to your notice. The mechanism is compact and strong. The piece was fired five hundred times in succession, partly divided between two mornings. There was but one failure to fire, supposed to be due to the absence of fulminate. In every other instance the operation was complete. The mechanism was not cleaned and yet worked throughout as at first. Not the least foulness on the outside, and very little within. The least time of firing seven rounds was ten seconds. I can recommend that a number of these pieces be introduced for trial in service.'[4]

This report was addressed to the Chief of Naval Ordnance Captain Andrew A. Harwood.

Two weeks later, on June 22, Captain Harwood wrote Charles Cheney at Hartford, Connecticut the following letter saying that the Navy would order seven hundred Spencer rifles.

'In consideration of the report made by Commander Dahlgren upon the magazine breech loading rifle, presented for trial by you, the bureau desires you to furnish with all practical dispatch for this department of the navy, the following quantity of the arms, together with the requisite amount of ammunition: 700 rifles. 70,000 ball cartridges. With the distinct understanding that the price of said arms and ammunition is not to exceed of that Sharp's rifle delivered at such naval stations, as the bureau may choose to appoint. And subjected to the visual inspection which prevails for small arms before the reception in the navy. You will please immediately notify the bureau of your acceptance of the above order under the condition stipulated. And you will likewise state at what time you will be able to supply the rifles in part or whole.'[5]

This order by the Navy would not in itself justify the vast capital needed for machinery to manufacture the Spencer. Therefore, the Cheney's next turned to the Army for additional orders. In August of 1861, Captain Alexander Dyer of the U.S. Army Ordnance Department tested the Spencer at Fort Monroe, Virginia.

'I fired the Spencer Repeating Rifle some eighty times. The loaded piece was then laid upon the ground and covered with sand, to see what would be the effect of getting sand into the joints. No clogging or other injurious effect appeared to have been produced. The lock and lower parts of the barrel were then covered with salt water and left exposed for twenty-four hours. The rifle was then loaded and fired without difficulty. It was not cleaned during the firing, and it appeared to work quite as well at the end as at the beginning.'[6]

In November of 1861, Major General McClellan (By Special Order No. 311) ordered a Board of Examination to test the Spencer rifle. The officers on this Board consisted of Captains Pleasanton, Sully and Lieutenant S.C. Bradford. On November 22, they met at the U.S. Arsenal in Washington, D.C. Their report had the following comments on the Spencer:

'In firing it is accurate; the range good; the charge used smaller than is generally used in small caliber; the cartridges, being in copper tubes, are less liable to damage. The rifle is simple and compact in construction, and less liable to get out of order than any other breech-loading arm now in use.'[7]

The durability of the Spencer was later shown in this letter from Crittenden & Tibbals addressed to the Spencer Repeating Rifle Company on September 10, 1864.

'GENTLEMEN: We send you, this day, the Rifle as requested, which we have had in constant use, at our works, since April, 1862, nearly two and a half years.

It has been fired more or less every day, by us and our men, for testing the cartridges, and by visitors who have been curious to try the arm.

This Rifle must have been fired at least Sixteen Thousand times. It has never been out of order or repaired. It has not been cleaned more than six times since we have had it, and it is now in good working order.

We have not taken any particular care of it, allowing almost any one to handle and fire it that wishes. . . P.S. We think the gun has not been cleaned more than three times.'[8]

A month after the November 22 trials, Warren Fisher, Jr. wrote to Secretary of War Simon Cameron proposing to manufacture ten

Christopher Miner Spencer

thousand Spencer repeating rifles with triangular bayonets at a cost of $40 each. Proposed deliveries were set for the first five hundred rifles in March of 1862 and thereafter one thousand for the months of April through November with the last one thousand five hundred in December. General Ripley accepted Fisher's proposals on December 26, 1861.

Spencer now had two government contracts and no factory. Charles Cheney came to the rescue by renting a portion of the Chickering & Sons Pianoforte building on Tremont Street in Boston which had been constructed in 1855.

The Spencer Repeating Rifle Company Articles of Incorporation were filed with the State of Massachusetts on January 27, 1862. The officers and directors were:

Joseph W. Clark, President
Warren Fisher, Jr., Treasurer
Charles Cheney, Director
Ward Cheney, Director
Rush Cheney, Director
Joseph W. Clark, Director[9]

Christopher Spencer sold his 1860 patent rights to Charles Cheney on May 10, 1861. Spencer did not have a financial interest in the company but was to receive a royalty of $1 for each gun sold.

The next problem for the Spencer Repeating Rifle Company occurred on January 29, 1862 when Secretary of War Stanton requested that all contractors of government orders send a copy of their contracts to Messrs. Holt and Owen. By February 5, Warren Fisher had sent his copy back to the commissioners. Meantime General Ripley requested that a sample pattern Spencer machine-made rifle be sent to the Ordnance Department for study. The rifle was delivered by Fisher on February 24, but was not officially approved until June 9.

On May 15, Holt and Owen informed Fisher that they were thinking of reducing the order for the Spencer or substituting them for the Springfield Rifle Musket. This brought a sharp protest from Fisher. Having invested vast sums of money for tooling up for the Spencer order, Fisher asked that the Government buy him out or at least pay for the cost so far incurred on this contract. He also proposed that the Government change the contract from rifles to carbines. The order, if approved, would then call for six thousand five hundred carbines in (56-56) and six thousand five hundred in .44 rimfire with deliveries starting in August.

The commissioners came to their final decision on the Spencer contract on May 31, 1862. They found that since the deliveries of March, April and May amounting to two thousand five hundred rifles had not been received; they would relieve the Government of the responsibility of having to take them. They left the balance of the order (7,500) to be delivered, with one thousand in June and one thousand in each additional month until the order was completed.

On June 19, 1862, Warren Fisher, Jr. and General Ripley entered into a new contract to reflect the deliveries of the seven thousand five hundred Spencer rifles authorized by Holt and Owen. This formal contract called for deliveries to start in July with one thousand and then one thousand additional rifles each month until completed. The price was set at $40 each. [10]

Many additional months of delay would pass before the first Spencer army rifles were ready for delivery; the first came on the last day of 1862 when five hundred Spencer rifles were received by the Ordnance Office. In January of 1863, an additional five hundred were received with one thousand two hundred in February; two thousand five hundred in April; one thousand five hundred in May and the remaining one thousand three hundred two in June for a total of seven thousand five hundred two Spencer rifles on the June 19 contract. [11]

As the Army order was being prepared for its initial deliveries in December 1862, the Navy sent Captain Chauncey and Mr. Griffith to Boston to inspect the rifles ordered by the Navy as part of the June 22, 1861 contract. On December 4, six hundred rifles were closely inspected before being crated for shipment. Chauncey's report of December 25 continues by saying:

'They were afterward fired, each rifle 10 times. The result has been most satisfactory in all respects, not only with respect to the arm itself, but also in reference to the ammunition, there having been but 4 failures of cartridges to explode in about 6,000 fires; being, I apprehend a much less percentage than in the case of the ordinary percussion cap.'[12]

NAVY PROCUREMENT OF SPENCER RIFLES[59]

CONTRACTOR'S OR SELLER'S NAME	DATE OF PURCHASE	QUANTITY OR KIND OF STORES	PRICE	AMOUNT	DATE OF CONTRACT OR ORDER
Spencer Repeating Rifle Co.	2/3/63	703 Spencer Rifles & Sword Bayonets	$43.00	$30,229.00	6/22/61
	8/18/63	100 Spencer Rifles without Bayonets	$38.00	$3,800.00	Purchase
	9/17/63	200 Spencer Rifles without Bayonets	$35.00	$7,000.00	Purchase
	8/27/67	6 Spencer Rifles with Sword Bayonets	$43.00	$258.00	Purchase
TOTAL		**1,009 Spencer Rifles**			

Out of the seven hundred barrels proof-tested, only one burst due to a flaw.[13] Ten Spencers were packed in each box with all the accompanying implements: Sword bayonets, brushes, cleaning rods, and screwdrivers.

Five days later, on December 30, Dahlgren wrote the Boston Navy Yard that six hundred Spencer rifles were to be delivered there and that they should be distributed into Naval services as follows: One hundred Spencer rifles to Rear Admiral Porter at Cario, Illinois; one hundred to Boston Naval Yard; two hundred to New York Naval Yard; fifty to Washington Naval Ordnance; one hundred to Fort Monroe; and fifty to Rear Admiral Farragut at Pensacola, Florida. Each Spencer rifle was to be issued with two hundred cartridges and a cartridge box. When they were issued, the receiving officers were to report on their reliability in actual naval service.[14]

On February 3, 1863 the Spencer rifles were received by the Naval Ordnance Departments when six hundred two were received at the Charlestown Naval Yard; one hundred rifles at the Philadelphia Navy Yard; plus one Spencer rifle to the U.S. Naval Academy at Newport, Rhode Island. Those seven hundred three Spencers were paid for at a cost of $43 each.[15]

The Navy's second order for Spencers came on August 18, 1863, when one hundred rifles were ordered without the bayonet. The price was set at $38 each with the deliveries made at the Washington Navy Yard. A month later on

September 17, two hundred more Spencer rifles were obtained with spare parts at a cost of $35 each.[16]

The first seven hundred three Spencer rifles received by the Navy were fitted to take the sword bayonet. The remaining three hundred rifles were of the Army pattern fitted to use the triangular bayonet.

The final delivery for the Navy did not occur until two years after the war, when on August 27, 1867, six Spencer rifles with sword bayonets were received at the Portsmouth Navy Yard. These six rifles cost the government $43 each. This last delivery had been placed to cover the following request from Gideon Wells, Secretary of the Navy:

'You will have prepared to be sent out in the Piscatagua as a present to the Prime Minister Siam, 6 Sharps breech loading rifles and 6 Spencer repeating rifles, with a suitable number of cartridges for each.'[17]

This delivery completed a total of one thousand nine Spencer rifles delivered to the U.S. Navy at a cost of $41,287.

The second Army contract for Spencers was the result of an order placed on July 13, 1863 by General Ripley requesting eleven thousand Spencer carbines at a cost of $25 each. This initial order for carbines saw its first delivery on October 3, 1863 when one thousand were received at the Ordnance Department. By year's end, seven thousand carbines had been delivered.

On September 24, 1863, the Spencer factory notified General Ramsay that they had two thousand rifles on hand that they had made for the State of Massachusetts, but would sell to the Government. Ramsay accepted this offer on September 28, with delivery being made on October 2. General Ramsay's reply to the Spencer company was:

'GENTLEMEN: I have to acknowledge the receipt of your letter of the 24th instant, stating that you have two thousand rifles on hand, made for the State of Massachusetts, but which you can turn over to this department. I have to inform you that this department will take the two thousand rifles, subject to the usual inspection, at the price of thirty-five dollars each, payments to be made on the usual certificates of inspection and receipt. These rifles are wanted for General Rosecrans and General Burnside, and should be delivered at once to the inspector of contract arms, who has been notified of this order.'[18]

With substantial deliveries being made, the Spencer Repeating Rifle Company and Christopher Spencer entered into a new royalty agreement on December 4, 1863. This new agreement called for Spencer to receive fifty cents for each gun sold to the Government and one dollar for each one sold to a private citizen.

The next order for Spencer rifles came on April 15, 1864 when the Ordnance Department requested delivery of one hundred rifles at $35, including appendages. The letter from Ramsay at the Ordnance Office to Warren Fisher, Jr. stated:

'SIR: Be pleased to furnish for the use of this department, and deliver at the factory where made, to Colonel Thornton, one hundred Spencer rifles, including appendages, and one hundred cartridge boxes. They are all to be subject to the usual inspection. You will be paid at the rate of thirty-five dollars ($35) for each rifle, including appendages, upon the usual certificates of inspection and receipt, in such funds as the Treasury Department may provide. Cartridge boxes and packing boxes extra.'[19]

On May 5, 1864 General Ramsay wrote to Govenor Andrew acknowledging Massachusetts cooperation in turning over its as yet undelivered Spencers to the Government saying:

'I have the honor to acknowledge the telegrams from General P.A. Pierce informing me that you have kindly consented to loan to this department eleven hundred and seventy-six Spencer carbines, and eighteen hundred and sixty-eight Spencer rifles, to be replaced by the same number during the present year. For this favor be pleased to accept my acknowledgments. Colonel Thornton has been instructed to receive these arms, and to give certificate for them, either to the Spencer Company or to such other person as you may think proper to facilitate this transaction, and will also see that the Spencer Company take measures to have these arms in due time.'[20]

Ramsay then wrote Warren Fisher:

'SIR: Colonel Thornton has been instructed to take immediate measures to receive and ship to New York arsenal the Spencer rifles and carbines turned over by State of Massachusetts.'[21]

These Spencers were delivered on May 14 and paid for at a rate of $35 each for the rifles and $30 each for the carbines.[22]

From December 31, 1862 to January 1, 1866, the Spencer Repeating Rifle Company furnished the U. S. Ordnance Office eleven thousand four hundred seventy-one Spencer rifles and sixty-four thousand six hundred eighty-five carbines at a cost of $2,078,427.29.[23]

There has been much speculation over the years that during the Civil War vast numbers of Spencer rifles and carbines were purchased privately from the factory. This is not supported, however, by the original ledger sheets from the Spencer Company which reveal that from 1864 to 1865 sundry sales show one thousand five hundred sixty-eight carbines, one hundred fifty-four rifles and twenty-four sporting rifles and carbines being sold. This is a rate of only about four percent of total sales to other than the ordnance office, fairly conclusive evidence of the lack of significant non-government sales.

The wartime Model 1860 Spencer rifles were .52 caliber. They had an overall length of forty-seven inches and weighed ten pounds. The unmarked lock is casehardened. The two piece stock is of black walnut. The thirty inch blued barrel has a brass blade front sight and single leaf, folding rear sight graduated to eight hundred yards. This sight is secured by a curved spring base. The army model takes the angular

A Union Cavalryman poses with his Spencer Rifle and other equipment. Note the bright polished saber scabbard, and the Model 1860 Colt. Like his companion on page 92 he has removed his revolver from its holster and thrust it through his belt where it would be more visible to the camera and the folks at home.
— Herb Peck Jr., collection

bayonet while the first seven hundred Spencers were of the navy pattern with the bayonet lug fastened to the bottom of the barrel for the sword bayonet. All Model 1860 Spencer rifles have six grooved rifling. The barrel is held to the forestock by three solid oval barrel bands. The case-hardened receiver is marked on the top part between breech and the barrel 'SPENCER REPEATING/RIFLE CO BOSTON MASS/-PAT'D MARCH 6, 1860.' To the rear of the breech is the serial number.

The sword bayonets for the Spencer Navy rifles have brass hilts. The overall length of the bayonet is twenty-four and three-quarter inches with a twenty and one-eighth inch blade. The serial number is found at the rear of the hilt. The manufacturer of this bayonet was Collins & Company of Hartford, Connecticut.

The first Spencer rifle to see combat did so in the hands of Sergeant Francis O. Lombard of Company 'F', lst Massachusetts Cavalry.[24] Lombard had enlisted at Springfield, Massachusetts on September 7, 1861 at the age of twenty-six. At the time of his enlistment, he was employed by Smith and Wesson. Prior to this time, he and Spencer had become friends and in the fall of 1862, Spencer sent him one of his hand-built repeaters, which he first put to use at Cumberland, Maryland on October 16, 1862 in a skirmish with the Confederate Cavalry. Lombard was given a field promotion to the rank of Second Lieutenant on May 30, 1863. While rescuing a wounded comrade at New Hope Church, Virginia, on November 27, 1863, Second Lieutenant Lombard was killed by a single enemy bullet. What became of his prized Spencer rifle remains a mystery.

The first one thousand Spencer rifles delivered to the U.S. Ordnance Department were sent by order of Major Hagner of the Ordnance office to Columbus, Ohio on January 19, 1863 for the use of the Ohio Sharpshooters.[25] At this time, the 5th, 6th and 7th Independent Companies of Ohio Sharpshooters were being organized at Camp Cleveland, Ohio. The rifles were used at the headquarters of Generals Rosecrans and Thomas.[26]

Captain Barber of the Ohio Sharpshooters wrote to the Spencer Rifle Company on November 8, 1863 about the Spencers' accuracy:

'I have just returned with my command from an expedition in which we have had a good opportunity to test our rifles with the rebel Sharpshooters. About six miles below Chattanooga the main road, over which supplies for the whole army must be drawn, lays along the banks of the Tennessee river, the south bank of which was held by the enemy, and their Sharpshooters played havoc with our teams and drivers. The river is 500 yards wide, I was ordered to protect the road. The 18th Ky., armed with the Enfield rifle, had been skirmishing with them for two days, and lost three men, and had no effect on the enemy. The first day we opened on them we killed two, wounded several, and drove them from every position along the river, we found by actual trial that our guns had longer range and greater accuracy. We seldom missed at 700 yards. I had 125 men with me, and for two weeks kept 600 reb's at bay, and, as I afterwards learned, killed and wounded over thirty, with a loss of one man wounded.

It was a genuine trial of arms, and resulted in proving the superiority of the Spencer Repeating Rifle over every other arm in the service.

Gen. Reynolds, Chief of Staff, said to me, 'It is the best rifle on the face of the earth,' and I am fully convinced that his remark is literally true.[27]

The Confederates also came to have great respect for these rifles as the following rather colorful anecdote illustrates:

"One day as our line of skirmishers were advancing one of the Johnnies yelled out-- 'helloa Yanks, have you got them d----d guns loaded to the muzzle again;' whilst the cavalry was picketing along Robertson's river, skirmishing was frequent along the line, but when our regiment took its turn we exchanged but a few shots with them when they offered the following proposition: —'say there, if you'ns won't shoot wee'ns won't shoot,' and peace existed along the lines as long as our regiment remained.'[28]

The first cavalry regiments to receive Spencer rifles were the 5th and 6th Michigan. They are the only regiments listed as having the Spencer as of March 31, 1863. The 5th is shown as having four hundred forty-nine Spencers and the 6th with two hundred sixty-seven.[29] At the Battle of Gettysburg three months later, on July

1-3, the 5th is listed with four hundred seventy-nine rifles while the 6th had but ninety-three Spencer rifles plus two hundred fifty-one Burnside carbines.[30] On the third day of Gettysburg, the Confederate cavalry led by Jeb Stuart fought a sharp cavalry battle with the Union cavalry east of Gettysburg. A portion of the Union cavalry led by General George Custer consisting of the lst, 5th, 6th and 7th Michigan Cavalry played a major role in the battle. The 5th and 6th Michigan were used as skirmishers and used their Spencer rifles with great effectiveness. The 5th actually ran out of ammunition during the battle. In this hotly contested cavalry battle, the Confederate losses were listed at one hundred eighty-one while the Union suffered two hundred fifty-four casualties of which eighty-four came from the 5th and 6th Michigan.

The first mounted infantry regiment to be supplied with Spencer rifles was Colonel John T. Wilder's Mounted Infantry Brigade. They were also the first to put them to combat use on a large scale.

Colonel Wilder organized his mounted infantry brigade during February and March of 1863. Wanting the best arms for his men, he first went to the New Haven Arms Company on March 20 and requested nine hundred Henry rifles. When they were unable to supply the Henry, Wilder turned to the seven shot repeating Spencer.

Colonel Wilder had met Christopher Spencer during Spencer's promotional tour of the Western battlefields in March 1863. Wilder proposed to purchase directly from the Spencer factory one thousand four hundred rifles to be paid individually by each soldier. He secured the necessary $50,000 by receiving promissory notes from each man and had his own bank send the money to Boston.

While the soldiers were willing to pay for their Spencers, it appears that the U.S. Ordnance Department stepped in and issued them their Spencers from those already delivered by the Spencer factory to the government.

Wilder's Brigade consisted of the 17th, 72nd Indiana, 92nd, 98th and 123rd Illinois. The 17th and 72nd Indiana were to receive their Spencers at Murfreesboro, Tennessee on May 15-17, 1863. The 98th Illinois Spencers were

General George A. Custer. Custers' 5th and 6th Michigan Cavalry were armed with Spencer rifles.   **National Archives**

delivered on May 31; while the 123rd Illinois were received on May 6. The 92nd, the last of the regiments to join Wilder's Brigade on July 10, were issued mounts and rifles about July 22.[31]

Wilder and his men did not have long to wait to put their Spencers to combat use. On June 24, 1863, while in the vanguard of General George Thomas' XIV Corps they held off repeated Confederate infantry attacks at Hoover's Gap. In these attacks Wilder was faced by General Stuart's infantry division. A newspaper account of this fight relates:

'Leaving this spur, which terminates one ridge of hills, and crossing a cornfield, Col. Jordan, with the 17th Indiana, took position in the woods crossing the second range of hills, while Col. Funkhouser, with the 98th Illinois, formed some distance to the right, on the same ridge. Soon after, the thunders of the artillery announced the opening of the battle, and the replies of the rebel gunners indicated a readiness to engage. Five regiments of rebel infantry rose from the

Colonel John T. Wilder whose Mounted Infantry brigade was the first to put their Spencer rifles to good use.   National Archives

low ground near the stream, and, cheering like men confident of easy victory, and disposed to inspire terror in their antagonists, came charging across the rolling but open field toward the 17th. The odds were heavily against us, but the boys, armed with the splendid Spencer Rifle, and true to the promptings of brave hearts that never flinched till beaten, coolly waited the auspicious moment.

The enemy approached within easy range, and received a tearing volley from the 17th, that checked but did not stay them. Supposing our guns exhausted, a cheer followed the report, and they moved on. Again the exhaustless weapons pour in their rain of bullets, and still the enemy press on. The rebels were nearing the line in largely superior force, and the Colonel looked anxiously for assistance. The bayonet might prolong the struggle, but ultimate capture seemed inevitable. Not a man left the line. Comrades were falling rapidly, but threatening disaster only nerved the men to greater exertion, and

they still bravely poured in their fire. Just as hope was giving way to despair, successive volleys on the right announced the arrival reinforcements, and the men took courage.

Col. Funkhouser, on a double quick, threw his regiment on the enemy's flank, and, with the same murderous Spencer Rifle, was mowing him at every volley, and moving forward, a perfect avalanche of destruction.

The enemy faltered, staggered back, and, as if furried to a decision by a united fire of the 98th and 17th, turned their backs and fled, leaving a large portion of their dead and wounded on the field.'[32]

The one-sided Union victory can be seen in the casualties of both sides. Wilder's killed were listed at forty-seven men while the number of Confederates lost is given at nearly five hundred.

At Chickamauga on September 20, 1863, Wilder's Lightning Brigade was to help slow down General Longstreet's devastating attack on the Union center. In these attacks, Wilder's Brigade was to sustain one hundred twenty-five casualties; but with the determination and skilled leadership of General Thomas, they were to keep the Union defeat from becoming a complete rout.

Ten days after the battle on September 30, when the quarterly ordnance reports were prepared, Wilder's regiments are shown with eighty percent of their arms as Spencers and the remainder muzzleloading rifles.

Wilder's Brigade
Armament on September 30, 1863[33]

Regiment	Spencer Rifles	Enfield Rifle Muskets	Colt Revolving Rifles	Springfield Rifle Muskets	Total
92nd Ill.	172	280			452
98th Ill.	354		9		363
123rd Ill.	262				262
17th Ind.	454			2	456
72nd Ind.	127	43		38	208
TOTAL	**1,369**	**323**	**9**	**40**	**1,741**

The overwhelming favor for the Spencer can be seen in the numerous reports forwarded to the Ordnance Department and to the Spencer factory. During the 1863-1864 Ordnance survey of breechloaders in Federal service, sixty-eight

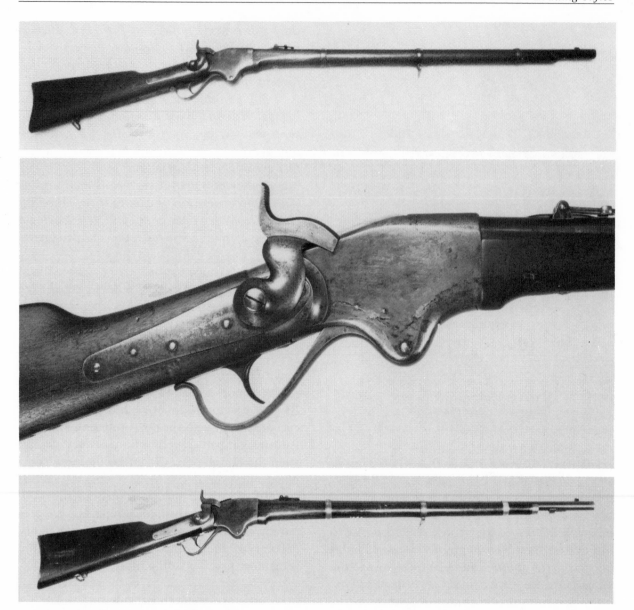

(top) The Spencer Repeating Rifle Company delivered 11,471 of the Army pattern rifles to the Ordnance Department between December 31, 1862 and October 26, 1864. This rifle, number 4779, is made to accept a conventional triangular bayonet.
                                                                                                                                  — Authors collection
(center) A close-up of the action of the Model 1860 Spencer repeater.
(bottom) One of the 700 Spencer Rifles delivered to the Navy on February 3, 1863. Note that in place of the triangular bayonet these rifles were fitted with a lug underneath the barrel to accept a saber bayonet. This is number 295.   — Roy Marcot collection

officers commented on the Spencer rifle. These officers rated it: fifty-seven as best arm in the service, three as very good and eight officers rated it as good.[34] Captain E.E. Sellers of Co. 'G' 98th Illinois rated it 'as the greatest arm in the Service,'[35] while Captain Oscar F. Bane of Co. 'A' 123rd Illinois Infantry stated they are 'superior to any weapon now made.'[36] These officers did raise the objections that the mainspring, rearsight and cartridge magazine spring had tendencies to break, and that the gun was too

heavy for mounted troops with the Spencer carbine being better suited for their service use.[37]

The Spencer factory received volumes of letters in praise of the effectiveness of their rifle, often from some of the most notable public figures. General George A. Custer wrote:

'Dear Sir: — Being in command of a Brigade of Cavalry which is armed throughout with the Spencer Carbine and Rifle, I take pleasure in testifying to their superiority over all other weapons. I am firmly of the opinion that fifteen

hundred men armed with the Spencer Carbine are more than a match for twenty-five hundred armed with any other fire-arm — I know this to be true from actual experiment.'[38]

On October 10, 1864 General U.S. Grant wrote:

'Dear Sir, — In reply to your letter of the 20th ult., requesting my opinion in regard to the merits of the Spencer Repeating arms, I have to say that it is the prevailing opinion amongst officers whose commands have been furnished with these weapons, that they are the best breech-loading arms now in the hands of troops, both as regards simplicity and rapidity in firing, and superiority of manufacture.'[39]

On July 26, 1865, shortly after the war had ended, Secretary of the Navy Gideon Welles wrote — taking credit for the Navy having introduced the Spencer to government service and remarking on President Lincolns interest in the Spencer.

'Sir,-- Your letter of the 14th inst., relative to the use of the Spencer Repeating Rifle in the Navy, has been received.

As you are aware, this rifle was first introduced into the public service through the agency of the Navy Department, after a very critical examination by the present Rear-Admiral Dahlgren, then having charge of the ordnance establishment in this city, and it gives me pleasure to state that the favorable opinion expressed by that officer in the examination has been fully sustained in service. Admiral Dahlgren has recently returned from the command, during the past two years, of one of the largest squadrons on the coast, and informs me that the Spencer Rifle was much sought after, and that officers once having it in use prefer it to any other. In one instance a boat's crew armed with this rifle were saved from capture, it not from death, by the rapidity with which they were enabled to deliver their fire.

I may also mention that the late President Lincoln, who took great interest in the different fire-arms, often expressed his satisfaction with the Spencer Rifle, and has more than once stated that he considered it the best arm in the service.'[40]

While the Spencer repeater was not in the Confederate inventory, a number of captured Spencer rifles were utilized. As early as Gettysburg (July 3, 1863), Sergeant W.O. Johnson of Co. 'C', 49th VA Infantry, was using a Spencer rifle in the fight around Culp's Hill. This rifle was probably captured from either the 5th or 6th Michigan Cavalry, since, at that time, they were the only troops in the Army of the Potomac equipped with it.

In mid-October, 1863, a supply wagon loaded with Spencer rifles and four thousand rounds of ammunition was captured by the Confederates near Decherd, Alabama. These and other captured Spencers fell into the hands of the 3rd and 8th Texas and the 4th Tennessee cavalry — all under the command of Major General Joseph 'Fighting Joe' Wheeler during the last year and a half of the war.[41]

In the East, Colonel John S. Mosby and his partisan rangers used both Colt revolvers and Spencer rifles and carbines. While many of the Southerners found ammunition for these rifles difficult to come by, this was no problem for Mosby since he found that Federal Ordnance depots were a good and easy source of supplies. He, therefore, put a number of them to use on their former owners. By November of 1864, Mosby had at least one hundred sixty-seven Spencers.

The South did not have the capacity to manufacture rimfire cartridges and lacked sufficient copper as well. What little copper the south possessed was used to fabricate percussion caps for their muzzle-loading rifle muskets. The Richmond Sentinel in their December 8, 1864 edition called for the Confederate government to manufacture Spencer ammunition for these rifles so that they could be used by the Southern cavalry to help 'remove that inequality between the opposing lines which tolled so heavily against us in the cavalry encounters in the past campaign.'[42]

If the Confederate infantry and cavalry did not have enough of a problem in combat, the Union forces were given even more firepower with the addition of the Blakeslee cartridge box. These new cartridge boxes were designed by Erastus Blakeslee of the First Connecticut Volunteer Cavalry and received U.S. Patent No. 45,469 on December 20, 1864. They were 'made of wood and covered with leather and are about

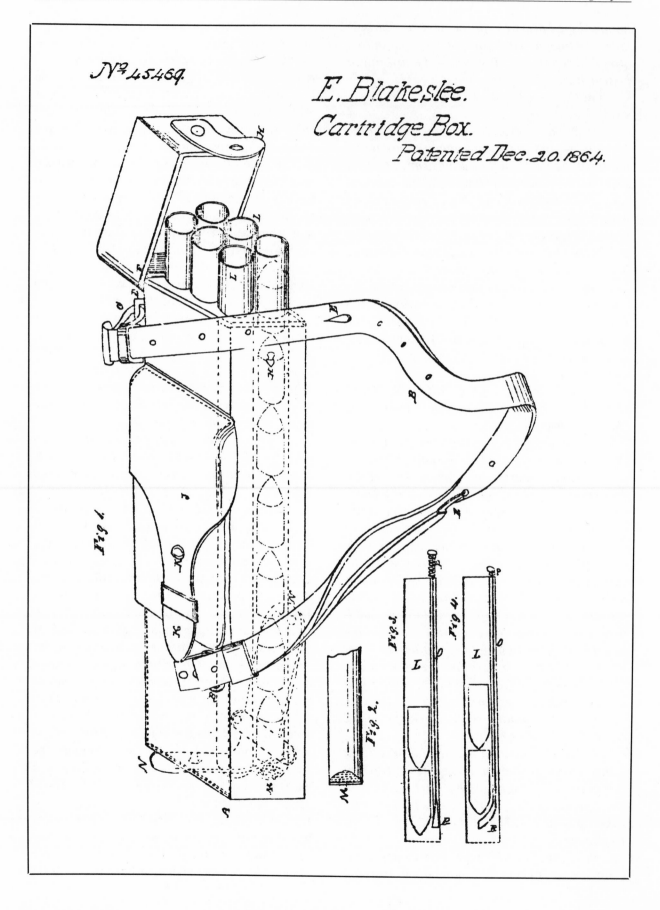

Nº 45469.

E. Blakeslee.
Cartridge Box.
Patented Dec. 20. 1864.

Fig. 1.

Fig. 2.

Fig. 3.

Fig. 4.

one foot in length and three by two inches square.'[43] The Blakeslee box 'consists in the combination of one or more metal tubes containing cartridges with a spring top cartridge-box and side pouch for pistol cartridges.'[44]

Each of the tubes were loaded with seven rimfire Spencer cartridges which the soldier would take from the cartridge box and pour into the Spencer for quicker loading. The actual claim made by Blakeslee in this patent read:

'The combination of one or more movable metal tubes, each containing two or more cartridges, with a spring-top cartridge-box and side pouch, as herein described and for the purposes set forth.'[45]

The first of these 'quickloaders', as the troops called them, held six tinned tubes with a capacity of forty-two rounds of Spencer ammunition. The Government, late in 1864, purchased five hundred of these six tube Blakeslee boxes from John Hammond of Washington, D.C.

The largest order for Blakeslee boxes was for the ten tube model made for cavalry use.

Between late 1864 and June 30, 1866, the Ordnance Department obtained thirty two thousand of these cartridge boxes at a cost of $153,036.[46] The manufacturers were Emerson Gaylord of Chicopee Falls, and W.H. Wilkinson of Springfield, Massachusetts.

Also, the Government purchased for infantry use one thousand thirteen-tube Blakeslee cartridge boxes. These were ordered from Emerson Gaylord on December 8, 1864 at a cost of $7.10 each for a total cost of $7,100.[47]

Since the Blakeslee box was a late arrival to the soldier in the field, they were to have little impact on the war's outcome. In the post-war years with the decline in the use of the Spencer, it appears that the Blakeslee boxes were discarded or left to collect dust in the Ordnance arsenals. In the 1907 Francis Bannerman catalog, surplus ten tube Blakeslee boxes sold for ninety cents each.

During the war a large number of regiments were armed at one time or another with the Spencer rifle. They included:

INFANTRY REGIMENTS[48]

7th Connecticut	72nd Indiana	79th New York
1st Delaware	97th Indiana	118th New York
9th Illinois	4th Kentucky	148th New York
27th Illinois	28th Kentucky	46th Ohio
92nd Illinois	37th Massachusetts	79th Ohio
98th Illinois	54th Massachusetts	75th Ohio Mounted Infantry
102nd Illinois	57th Massachusetts	Ohio Sharpshooters
123rd Illinois	14th Michigan	105th Pennsylvania
13th Indiana	24th Michigan	148th Pennsylvania
17th Indiana	27th Michigan	190th Pennsylvania
20th Indiana	3rd New Hampshire	2nd U.S. Sharpshooters
39th Indiana	10th New Hampshire	37th U.S. Colored Infantry
40th Indiana	65th New York	

CAVALRY REGIMENTS[49]

8th Indiana	5th Michigan	10th Michigan
11th Kentucky	6th Michigan	5th New York
2nd Massachusetts	7th Michigan	7th New York
4nd Massachusetts	8th Michigan	11th Ohio
2nd Michigan	9th Michigan	1st West Virginia

ARMY PROCUREMENT OF SPENCER RIFLES[60]

CONTRACTOR'S OR SELLER'S NAME	DATE OF PURCHASE	QUANTITY OR KIND OF STORES	PRICE	AMOUNT	DATE OF CONTRACT OR ORDER
Spencer Repeating Rifle Co.	12/31/62	500 Spencer rifles & appendages	$40.00	$20,000.00	6/19/62
	1/17/63	500 Spencer rifles & appendages	$40.00	$20,000.00	6/19/62
	2/23/63	1,200 Spencer rifles & appendages	$40.00	$48,000.00	6/19/62
	4/13/63	1,500 Spencer rifles & appendages	$40.00	$60,000.00	6/19/62
	4/22/63	500 Spencer rifles & appendages	$40.00	$20,000.00	6/19/62
	4/29/63	500 Spencer rifles & appendages	$40.00	$20,000.00	6/19/62
	5/9/63	500 Spencer rifles & appendages	$40.00	$20,000.00	6/19/62
	5/19/63	500 Spencer rifles & appendages	$40.00	$20,000.00	6/19/62
	5/30/63	500 Spencer rifles & appendages	$40.00	$20,000.00	6/19/62
	6/9/63	500 Spencer rifles & appendages	$40.00	$20,000.00	6/19/62
	6/16/63	500 Spencer rifles & appendages	$40.00	$20,000.00	6/19/62
	6/29/63	302 Spencer rifles & appendages	$40.00	$12,080.00	6/19/62
	6/29/63	Cost of Material Furnished in proving 7,510 barrels. ($113.79) Less cost of inspection of 1,664 barrels. (22.75)		$91.04	
	10/2/63	2,000 Spencer rifles & appendages	$35.00	$70,000.00	9/28/63
	4/22/64	100 Spencer rifles & appendages	$35.00	$3,500.00	4/15/64
	5/14/64	1,868 Spencer rifles & appendages	$35.00	$65,380.00	5/7/64
	10/26/64	1 Spencer rifle & appendages	$35.00	$35.00	10/15/64
	3/13/65	Material used in proving 48,055 carbines & rifle barrels. Cost of inspection 5,410 carbine & rifle barrels.		$1,008.18	
Schuyler, Hartley & Graham	8/1/63	1 Spencer rifle		$40.00	Purchase

TOTAL   11,472 Spencer Rifles

In the post war years although the Spencer carbine saw substantial frontier use in the hands of the cavalry, the Spencer rifle was to see little use. However, in June 1866, the llth Ohio Cavalry located at Fort Leavenworth had on hand twenty-seven Spencer rifles, three Merrill rifles plus thirty-three Joslyn carbines and one hundred eighteen Spencer carbines.[50] As late as March 31, 1871, the 3rd U.S. Cavalry in the Arizona Territory still had five Spencer rifles plus the 50/70 Sharps carbine and Springfield rifle in 50/70.[51] To maintain the Spencer in

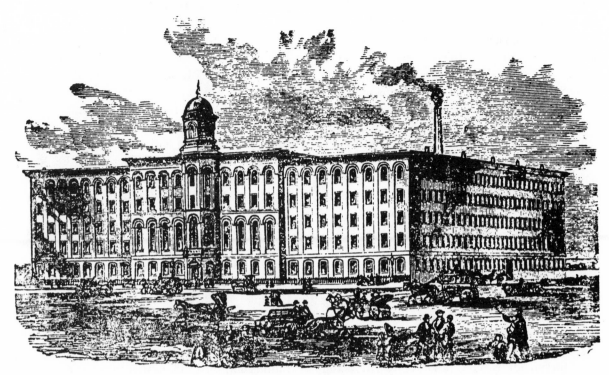

THE SPENCER ARMORY
1862 - 1868

good working order, repairs were performed at the Springfield Armory. Between July 1866 and June 1869, nine thousand seven hundred seventy-eight Spencer carbines and one thousand two hundred fifteen Spencer rifles were repaired at the Armory.[52]

Of the one thousand three rifles purchased by the U.S. Navy during the war, eight hundred forty-seven remained in inventory on December 31, 1866 located at various naval installations as follows:[53]

Portsmouth	11
Boston	45
New York	211
Philadelphia	124
Washington D. C.	260
Jefferson Barracks	139
Pensacola	57

The wartime Spencer rifles (M1860) were not equipped with the Stabler cut-off device. This device allowed the rifle to be fired as a single-shot holding the cartridges in the butt-stock as a reserve. This invention of Edward Stabler of Maryland will be found on many of the post war carbines and rifles and on all Spencer repeaters refinished by the Springfield Armory.

Naturally, the firearms business in the post war years was in a general decline. Between 1865 and 1868 only forty-three thousand eight hundred arms of all types were manufactured at the Spencer factory. Of this total, eighteen thousand nine hundred fifty-nine Model 1865 Spencer carbines were delivered to the Ordnance Department between April 1865 and January 1, 1866. The remaining twenty-four thousand eight hundred forty consisted of commercial sales or arms sold to foreign governments. This was not sufficient volume to keep the company solvent. In October of 1868 the Spencer Repeating Rifle Company sold all of its assets to the Fogerty Rifle Company of Boston. On August 6, 1869, Oliver Winchester of the Winchester Repeating Arms Co. purchased the assets of Fogerty and then on September 29, 1869 sold at auction all of the Spencer machinery for $138,000. On August 22, 1870, Christopher Spencer signed an agreement with Winchester to assign all future patents or improvements in repeating rifles to Winchester.

After the war the government sold large amounts of small arms to private citizens. The majority of Spencers were sold between January 1, 1869 and June 6, 1871. During this time frame, thirty-five thousand two hundred thirty-eight Spencer carbines and one thousand three hundred eighty rifles were sold.[54]

As an example, a sale of Spencer rifles occurred in November of 1870 when eight hundred were sold to Caleb Huse, and in January of 1871 when five hundred eighty sold to Thomas Richardson. In both of these transactions Spencer rifles brought $30 each![55]

On June 5, 1865 the Ordnance Department *'directed volunteers, going out of service, might if they so desired, retain their arms, upon the value thereof being charged to them on the muster rolls, they can now do so at the following rates: . . . Spencer carbines and Rifles, with or without accoutrements, $10.00'*[56]

By this method, two thousand eight hundred forty-four Model 1860 Army rifles and eight thousand two hundred eighty-nine Model 1860 carbines were sold.[57]

In addition, the Ordnance Office transferred to the States for their militias' use 681 Spencers. Of these Ohio received 30 rifles on 2/13/67, the Colorado Territory; 500 rifles on 10/16/68, Indiana; 150 rifles on 5/14/73 and the State of Maine received 1 rifle on 11/3/75.[58]

After the war, Christopher Spencer left the Spencer Repeating Rifle Co. and became associated with Sylvester Roper and the Roper Repeating Rifle Company. By 1872, it was known as the Billings and Spencer Company of Hartford, Connecticut.

Spencer's most important patent after the Civil War came in 1874 when he developed the first automatic screw machine and with this idea, he founded the Hartford Machine Screw Company in 1876. He sold out in 1882. By May 9, 1883, he formed the Spencer Arms Company to manufacture the first practical pump action shotgun. This company was sold to Francis Bannerman in 1888. Christopher Spencer died on January 14, 1922.

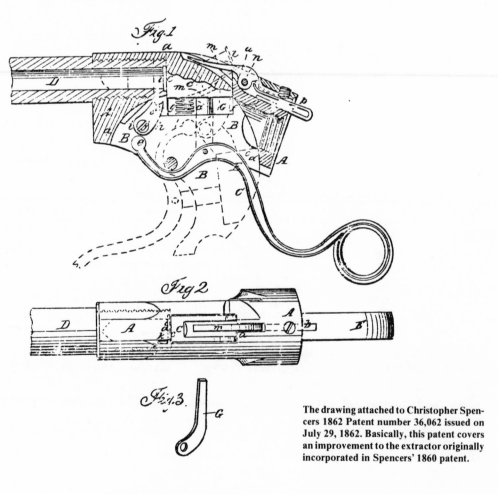

The drawing attached to Christopher Spencers 1862 Patent number 36,062 issued on July 29, 1862. Basically, this patent covers an improvement to the extractor originally incorporated in Spencers' 1860 patent.

[1]U.S. Patent Office, U.S. Patent No. 27,393, March 6, 1860.
[2]Ibid, U.S. Patent No. 36,062, July 29, 1862.
[3]Ibid.
[4]NARG 74, Section 145.
[5]NARG 74, Section 6.
[6]L.D. Satterlee, *10 Old Gun Catalogs, Spencer Catalog,* Chicago 1962, p. 4.
[7]Ibid.
[8]Ibid, p. 19.
[9]Robert A. Gussman & Ransom E. Lindsay, *Spencer Repeating Rifle Company,* Gun Report, January, 1967, p. 15 & 16.
[10]Executive Document No. 99, 40th Congress 2nd Session
[11]Ibid.
[12]Satterlee, op. cit. p. 31
[13]Ibid.
[14]NARG 74, Section 3.
[15]NARG 74, 158.
[16]Ibid.
[17]NARG 74, Section 3.
[18]Executive Document No. 99, 40th Congress 2nd Session.
[19]Ibid.
[20]Ibid.
[21]Ibid.
[22]Ibid.
[23]Ibid.
[24]Roy Marcot, Christopher Spencer's 'Yankee Lighting', *America, The Men and Their Guns That Made Her Great,* Los Angeles, 1981. p. 60.
[25]NARG 156, Section 118.
[26]Frederick H. Dyer, *A Compendium of the War of the Rebellion,* Vol. II, Dayton, 1978, p. 1495.
[27]Satterlee, op. cit. p. 14.
[28]Ibid.
[29]NARG 156, Section 110.
[30]Ibid.
[31]John D. McAulay, *Spencer Rifles for Wilder's Brigade at Chickamauga,* The Gun Report, January 1980, p. 69.
[32]Chicago Evening Journal; July 16, 1863.
[33]NARG 156, Section 111.
[34]NARG 156, Section 215.
[35]Ibid.
[36]Ibid.
[37]Ibid.
[38]Satterlee, op. cit. p. 16.
[39]Ibid, p. 20.
[40]Ibid, p. 25.
[41]Wayne R. Austerman, *The Spencer in Confederate Service,* Arm Gazette, September 1980, p. 21-25.
[42]The Richmond Sentinel, December 8, 1864.
[43]U.S. Patent Office, U.S. Patent No. 45,469, December 20, 1864.
[44]Ibid.
[45]Ibid.
[46]Roy M. Marcot, *The Blakeslee 'Quick-Loader',* Man At Arms, March/April 1982, p. 21.
[47]ibid, p. 22.
[48]NARG 156, Section 111.
[49]NARG 156, Section 110.
[50]Ibid.
[51]Ibid.
[52]Roy Marcot, *Springfield Armory Conversions & Repairs to Spencer Repeating carbines,* The Gun Report, July 1980, p. 66.
[53]Rollin V. Davis, M.D., *The Spencer 'Navy' Rifle,* The Gun Report, August 1974, p. 19.
[54]NARG 156, Section 125.
[55]Ibid.
[56]Circular No. 13 - Series of 1865.
[57]Roy Marcot, *Spencer Firearms On The Western Frontier,* The Texas Gun Collector, Spring 1983, p. 13.
[58]NARG 156, Section 118.
[59]NARG 74, Section 158.
[60]Executive Document No. 99, 40th Congress, 2nd Session

B. F. JOSLYN.

Breech-Loading Fire-Arm.

No. $\left\{\begin{array}{l} 2,431, \\ 33,435. \end{array}\right\}$ Patented Oct. 8, 1861.

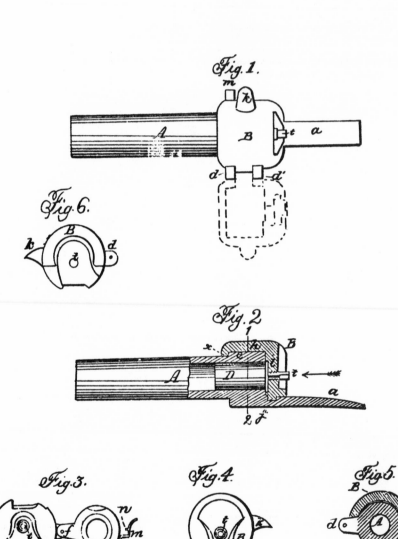

Fig. 1.

Fig. 6.

Fig. 2.

Fig. 3.   Fig. 4.   Fig. 5.

Witnesses { Charles Howson
            Charles E. Foster

Henry Howson
Atty for B. F. Joslyn

THE SPRINGFIELD JOSLYN RIFLE

The first mass production of breechloaders at the U.S. Springfield Armory occurred in early 1865 with the introduction of the Springfield Joslyn Rifle. These rifles are not conversions of muzzleloading Springfield rifle muskets but are, in fact, the first true breechloaders manufactured at the Springfield Armory.

What sets this Springfield rifle apart from a conversion is that it was manufactured in .50 caliber — to take the .56-.50 Spencer cartridge — not made from a .58 caliber rifle musket barrel bored out and sleeved to .50 caliber. In addition, the forty-eight inch walnut stock was specially manufactured at the Springfield Armory to take the Joslyn breech action as was standard on the Model 1864 Joslyn carbine. Plus, these rifles were equipped with a reshaped side-hammer bent well over the stock in order to reach the firing pin. The special shaped lockplate is marked forward of the hammer with: U.S. SPRINGFIELD and to the rear the date 1864.

These Springfield Joslyns weigh nine pounds eight ounces with an overall length of fifty-two inches. The thirty-five and one-half inch barrel finished in the bright has an iron blade front sight and a single leaf rearsight graduated to five hundred yards. The barrel is unmarked.

The three solid oval barrel bands retained by the conventional band springs forward of the bands, triggerguard, 'US' marked buttplate and knurled slotted type ramrod used on the Springfield Joslyn were also standard on the Model 1864 Springfield Rifle Musket then in production at the Armory.

The Joslyn breech action used on these rifles is fitted with a knurled button release. This knurled release knob works by being pulled out against spring tension which, in turn, releases the breechblock to swing up and over on its hinges to the left. This motion exposes the chamber for the inserting of the .56-.50 Spencer rimfire cartridge. The breechblock is then returned to its closed position for firing. The .56-.50 Spencer rimfire cartridge had an overall length of 1.56 inches. The .52 diameter bullet weighed three hundred fifty grains and the cartridge contained a powder charge of forty-five grains.

The Joslyn breechblock is also fitted with a gas vent and a protective firing pin shield. The only mark on the top of the breech is the serial number such as M1963. The rear face of the breech-cap is marked: B.F. JOSLYN'S PATENT /OCT 8 1861 JUNE 24 1862, in two lines. The serial number will be found on the casehardened breech tang.

Benjamin F. Joslyn of Worcester, Massachusetts, the designer of this breech action, received his patent for this design on October 8, 1861 with U.S. Patent No. 33,435. His improvements in firearms consist, '*First, in a breech hinged to the end of the barrel and constructed substantially as set forth hereinafter, so that its upper portion may fit over an enlargement on the end of the barrel in a manner which renders the said breech incapable of moving longitudinally when the cartridge is discharged; secondly, in a device, described hereinafter, for retaining the lower portion of the breech in its proper position in respect to the end of the barrel; and, thirdly, in a device for locking the breech to the barrel and readily releasing it therefrom.*'[1]

Additional improvements were made by Joslyn to the breech-cap by designing an extractor system. This system was covered by U.S. Patent No. 35,688 of June 24, 1862. Joslyn stated, '*My improvement consists in a curved wedge-formed projection combined with and arranged on the movable breech of the said*

B. F. JOSLYN.
Breech-Loading Fire-Arm.

No. 35,688.   Patented June 24, 1862.

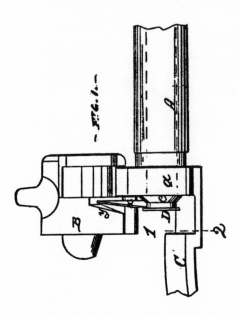

Witnesses { Charles E foster
{ Charles Howson

Henry Howson
Atty for B. F. Joslyn

firearm . . . so that the metallic cartridge may be partly withdrawn from the barrel during the act of throwing back the movable breech.'[2] The inclined side of the projection of the breechblock would seat the cartridge upon the closing of the breech and upon opening the breech the inclined plane extracted the cartridge a short distance so that it could easily be removed by the finger and thumb.

Both of these patents — of October 8, 1861 and June 24, 1862 — are employed on all production M1862 and M1864 Joslyn carbines as well as the Springfield Joslyn rifles.

The U.S. Navy was the first to test Joslyn's new breechloading design. On May 20 and June 14, 1861, they tested a Joslyn carbine with fair success. Later, on October 5, 1861, and again on July 28, 1862, a Joslyn rifle musket was tested by the Navy. In the July 28 test, a .58 caliber rifle with a thirty and one-quarter inch barrel was fired five hundred times and afterwards examined. The rifle was found to be in good condition except for considerable amount of leading in the barrel. The Navy's basic objection to the Joslyn rifle was that the metallic cartridge cases could not be used a second time and that the Joslyn musket could not use the common ammunition then in use with the rifle-musket.[3] No further testing of the Joslyn appears to have been conducted by the Navy.

The Army's first test of the Joslyn occurred on June 19, 1862 at West Point, New York. In this test two carbines were test fired by Captain S.V. Benet with very good results. The U.S. Ordnance Department eventually purchased ten thousand two hundred one Joslyn rimfire carbines between May 1, 1863 and February 25, 1865 at a cost of $243,028.[4]

By the fall of 1864, the Springfield Armory had designed the new .56-.50 Spencer rimfire cartridge which was to become the standard U.S. cartridge. Earlier on May 19, 1864, Major Dyer had written General Ramsay that he had test fired the Model 1864 Joslyn carbine several thousand times and found them as little liable to get out of order as any breechloader that he had fired. These facts seem to have a positive result on the government since on December 6, 1864, Major T.T.S. Laidley Commanding Officer at the Springfield Armory wrote the Joslyn Firearms Company, Stonington, Connecticut, asking if they would furnish two or three thousand breech-caps and tang pieces for their carbines. The letter continues by giving the reasons for their requesting the Joslyn breechblocks, *'It is desirable to put two or three thousand breechloading muskets into service as soon as practicable, and I am directed to get them up if it is possible. It can only be done by your supplying these parts. A price will be paid you to cover your royalty if you will furnish them. It is intended to make the muskets .50 in cal.'*[5]

Joslyn wrote back on December 22, 1864 stating that they could make the deliveries. However, they requested *'a few shells or cartridges for the new model musket and . . . tang screw for the purpose of counter sinking the hole in the tang.'*[6] On February 23, 1865 Joslyn was able to write the Springfield Armory that they had sent one hundred sixty caps and tangs on February 16 and another three hundred sixty as of that date and by March 18 a total of six hundred caps and tangs had been sent.[7] It appears at about this time Joslyn wrote to General Dyer at the Ordnance Department stating that he had additional breechblocks which he could supply the government. On April 12, Dyer gave the following directions to Major Laidley at Springfield, *'The Joslyn Company has a number of breech-caps and tangs on hand which may answer for the muskets you are making. You may do well to purchase them and to continue the manufacture of those muskets until not less than 5,000 shall have been made.'*[8] While this letter of April 12 gave the go ahead for the manufacture of five thousand rifles, only three thousand and seven rifles were made between January and June of 1865.

These rifles were issued to the 5th and 8th U.S. Veteran Volunteer Infantry regiments for field tests. Both of these regiments were organized at Camp Stoneman, Washington, D.C. between January and April of 1865 and issued their Springfield Joslyns after April of 1865. These rifles did not see combat use due to their late arrival in the field. As late as June 1866, the 5th U.S. Veteran Volunteer Infantry located at Fort Wood, New York was listed with fifty-two Springfield Joslyn while the 8th U.S. Veteran Volunteer Infantry was listed with twelve.[9]

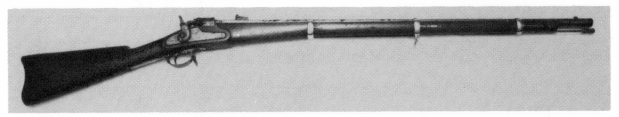

(above and left) The Springfield Joslyn Rifle — the first breechloader mass produced at the Springfield Armory. At the left are close-up views of the Joslyn breech open, closed and shown from above. This rifle is serial number M1963.   **— Authors collection**

A much more extensive testing of the Springfield Joslyn occurred in July of 1867. By Special Order No. 126 of June 5, 1867, a Board of Examination was to convene at the New York State Arsenal in New York City on July 9 at 10:00 a.m. The Board's task was to test the various methods of converting the Springfield Rifle Musket to breechloading from muzzle-loading. In addition to testing the Joslyn conversion of the Springfield Rifle Muskets, the Board of Examination tested the conversions of Allin, Mont Storm, Roberts, Peabody, Miller, Needham, Remington, Sharps and Labuire.

The Springfield Joslyn musket, .50 caliber with a twenty-eight inch barrel, was entered by William Herrick of New York City. Each of the conversion systems underwent a battery of ten tests. In the first test the Joslyn was fired ninety-five times in a span of seven minutes and forty-five seconds. In one minute, Benjamin Joslyn fired it ten times with eight hitting the target. A private soldier was able to fire it eight times in a minute. With the standard .56-.50 Spencer cartridge the bullet penetrated eleven boards. The Joslyn was disassembled in forty seconds and reassembled in one minute.[10]

While the Springfield Joslyn test results were very favorable, no additional arms were converted to this system. The government was to stay with the Allin conversions which deve-loped into the 'trapdoor' Springfield. In early 1871, one thousand six hundred Joslyns made at the Springfield Armory in 1865 were now converted to take the 50/70 centerfire cartridge. These Springfield Joslyn rifles were converted by rechambering, plugging the original firing pin hole and fitting a new firing pin in the middle of the breechblock. These rifles are found with mixed serial numbers.

In February of 1871, all one thousand six hundred of the 50/70 Springfield Joslyn rifles were sold by the government to Thomas Richardson for $15.50 each. At this same time, Richardson also purchased ten thousand Springfield .50 caliber trapdoor rifles at $21.60 each.[11] These arms were then sent to France for the Franco-Prussian War. It is believed that the Springfield Joslyn rifles were captured by the Germans and in turn were sold by them to Belgium. Here, they were converted to shotguns for use in Africa.

The U.S. Government was still selling these rifles as late as December 23, 1892 when fifteen were sold at a price of $1 each.[12] The 1907 Francis Bannerman catalog listed these rifles at a price of $3.85.

While the Springfield Joslyn rifles arrived on the scene to late to play a role in winning the war for the Union, they have their place in U.S. firearms history being the first mass-produced breechloaders made at Springfield.

[1]U.S. Patent Office, U.S. Patent No. 33,435 of October 8, 1861.
[2]U.S. Patent Office, U.S. Patent No. 35,688 of June 24, 1862.
[3]NARG 74-145.
[4]John D. McAulay, *Carbines of the Civil War 1861-1865,* Union City: 1981, p. 75.
[5]Arthur F. Nehrbass, *The Springfield Joslyn Rifle,* The American Rifleman, December 1972, p. 28.
[6]Ibid.
[7]Ibid p. 29.
[8]Andrew F. Lustyik, *The Joslyn Carbine,* The Gun Report, September 1962, p. 18.
[9]NARG 156-111.
[10]C.E. Fuller, *The Breech-Loader in the Service 1816-1917,* New Milford: 1965, p. 277.
[11]NARG 156-124.
[12]NARG 156-125.

W. M. STORM.

Breech-Loading Fire-Arm.

No. 15,307.   Patented July 8, 1856.

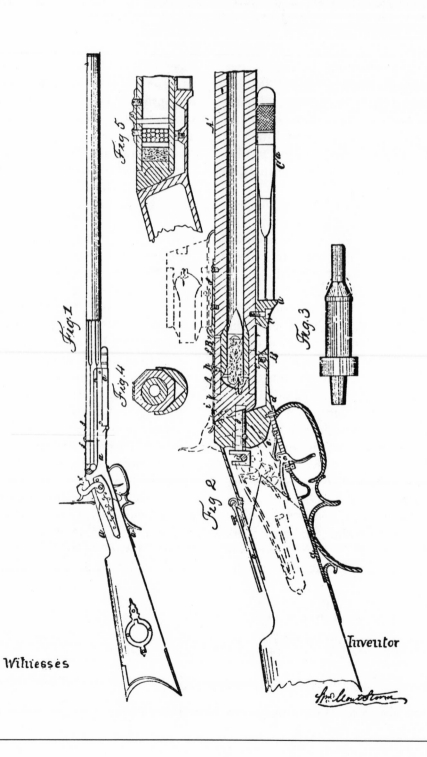

Witnesses

Inventor

ALTERATIONS TO BREECHLOADING 1857-1861

In the early 1850's, Congress became interested in having the Ordnance Department conduct test trials of the various breech-loading designs for possible future military service. Toward this goal, Congress on August 5, 1854 appropriated the sum of $90,000 for the purchase of the best breech-loading rifles in the opinion of the Secretary of War for the use of the United States Army. The then Secretary of War, Jefferson Davis, and his administration were not in favor of breechloaders and were of the opinion that the muzzleloading rifles were the superior arm for infantry use. So it is not surprising that at the end of Jefferson Davis's term, March 4, 1857, the balance of $82,143.50 remained unspent.

The new Secretary of War, John B. Floyd, took a different view from Davis and proceeded with the testing of the various breech-loading patterns. During his term in office, a number of Joslyn, Maynard, Burnside and Sharps carbines were purchased and issued to the cavalry. Also under his direction, a number of muskets and rifles were altered to the breech-loading designs of Mont Storm and Morse which utilized metalic cartridges as well as the more conventional percussion ignition Lindner and Merrill.

MONT STORM

William Mont Storm of New York City received his U.S. patent No. 15,307 dated July 8, 1856 for his improvements in breech-loading firearms. The Mont Storm breech is similar in appearance to that of the 'trap door' Allin Conversion with a small rounded handle mounted on the right side of the breechblock. To operate this action:

'Lift the hammer to full-cock, and 'e' is withdrawn just clean of 'b'. While the thumb still rests upon the hammer, the forefinger is hooked under the enlarged head of the usual vent-screw, (generally cut off smooth,) and the charge-chamber is lifted out of its bearings and thrown over upon the top of the barrel in the position shown by the dotted lines, Fig. 2, its muzzle directly facing the operator, and clear of everything for the convenient insertion of the cartridge. The chamber may then be thrown back to its original position, and the trigger may be pulled for discharge. If the chamber was not exactly home to its bearings, the bolt 'e' brings it so as the hammer commences to fall, the forward end of 'e' being tapered for that purpose. As the explosion takes place, the portion of the charge first ignited being in the rear of the tubular bolt-valve B, where its annular area is exposed for this purpose, together with the friction of the ball, particularly if a minie, spreading out in firm contact with the bore of the tube, forces and holds the bolt-valve firmly forward in its seat and across the joint, locking down the forward end of the chamber and perfectly tightening the joint, while the bolt 'e' locks down the rear end of the chamber. To prevent any leak past the rear or side of the tube, it is there edged with a softer metal, which expands with the discharge on the principle of the minie-ball, but at the same time not preventing it (B) from moving bodily forward to press into its seat firmly by the force of the explosion.'[1]

Mont Storm had twelve claims upon which he was requesting his patent of which the following are the most significant:

1. A charge chamber which swings out of the line of the bore on a hinge, in combination with a fixed recoil seat.

2. A tapered chamber face to align the chamber with the bore.

3. A chamber sleeve (bolt-valve) which is

driven forward by the explosion of the charge to seal the breech joint.

4. The arrangement of the hinge on top.[2]

On August 17, 1857, a Board of Officers met at West Point, New York to test various breechloaders to find those arms most suited for military use. Mont Storm presented two converted muzzleloading arms for testing. Unfortunately for him, both of his guns broke down during testing. The Board eventually reported in favor of the Burnside carbine.

The following year Secretary of War John Floyd appointed a board to proceed to West Point to examine all methods of altering muzzleloading arms to breechloading. The board met at West Point on July 22, 1858 and found favor of George Morse's design which used a special metallic cartridge. During these test trials, Mont Storm had a rifle and two muskets converted to his design tested by the Board. Both rifle and musket performed well and were favorably received by the Board.

Due to these test results, the Government purchased from Mont Storm, on September 22, 1858, the right to alter two thousand arms to his pattern design. In 1859, four hundred arms were altered to the Mont Storm pattern at the Harpers Ferry Arsenal.

In September of 1859 Harpers Ferry sent two Mont Storm altered rifles to the Washington Navy Yard for the Navy to test. During these tests, William Foreman represented the inventor. In a letter dated September 24 he wrote that the Navy fired a .58 caliber rifle twenty-seven times and a .54 caliber rifle five times with 'very considerable escape of gas from the function of the chamber and barrel - attributed to imperfect connection of the parts.'[3] Because of the above problems, testing was halted until further directions were received. Further tests were performed on October 18 with similar problems, 'the location of the vent, the cap would not set off the charge because of the vent location.'[4]

Three days later Franklin Buchanan, Chief of Ordnance at the Washington Navy Yard, gave these directions: *You will discontinue the firing of these arms and have them carefully packed in the boxes in which they were sent to this yard and hold them subject to the orders of* *the Ordnance Department of the Army.'*[5]

While the latter post Civil War Mont Storm actions were used with rimfire ammunition, these pre-war arms were made to use the percussion ignition system. The .58 caliber arms using the Mont Storm alterations used a 0.61 inch diameter bullet which weighed four hundred eighty grains. The powder charge was sixty grains with the overall length of 1.92 inches.

At the outbreak of the War Between the States in 1861, the Confederate forces in April 1861 captured and burned the rifle works at Harpers Ferry. It appears of the four thousand two hundred eighty-seven arms destroyed in this fire all four hundred Mont Storm arms were among them accounting for the fact that no trace of these altered Mont Storm arms is known to exist today.

During the Civil War, Captain Silas Crispin at the New York Arsenal, with the go-ahead from General Ripley, ordered two thousand Mont Storm carbines on March 11, 1862 from Schuyler, Hartley and Graham of New York City at a price of $26.50 each. These carbines were to be used by the State of Indiana. By the end of the year 1862, five hundred Mont Storm carbines were completed; but since the delivery time on the contract had expired, the Ordnance Department would not accept them. To whom Schuyler, Hartley and Graham sold these carbines is unknown. It appears that these carbines were manufactured by Charles R. Alsop of Middletown, Connecticut. There was no further use of the Mont Storm design during the war.

MORSE

The most advanced alteration was the Morse design. These arms were the first to use a centerfire cartridge and the first breechloaders manufactured at the Springfield Armory.

George W. Morse of Baton Rouge, Lousiana, received U.S. Patent No. 15,995 of October 28, 1856 for his improvement in breech-loading firearms. His patent claims were:

'1. Inserting the rim N, or its equivalent, without contact into the chamber O, substantially in the manner and for the purpose described, contact being attained through the medium of a cartridge-case.

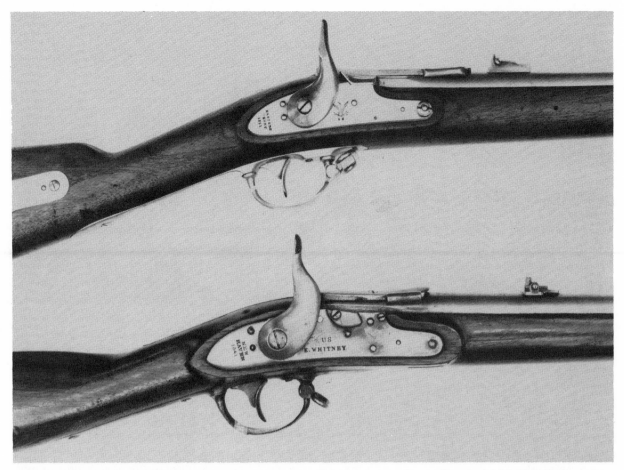

(top) The Morse breech loading system was the first military conversion to use a centerfire cartridge. (top) A Model 1841 rifle made at Harper's Ferry and later converted to the Morse system. (bottom) An Eli Whitney musket, originally a flintlock, which has been both converted to the Morse system and cut down to carbine length. — **Milwaukee Public Museum collection**

2. The nippers 's' and the mode of operating them by the pins 'r' and the shoulder 7 on the hammer, or equivalents therefor, substantially in the manner and for the purpose described.

3. The combination of movable parts, or their equivalents, whereby I retract or deliver the gun of a cartridge, drop it, open and clear the way for the insertion of another cartridge, whether the previous charge was fired or failed to fire, and cock the hammer automatically at one motion, substantially in the manner described.'[6]

Additional improvements were made to Morse's design which were covered by U.S. Patent No. 20,503 of June 8, 1858. In this letter patent Morse states:

'My invention relates to that class of firearms which are loaded at the breech, and which are adapted to the use of a metallic cartridge-case; and it consists in combining and arranging

a percussion-rod in a movable breechpiece with a sliding bolt, so that the lock in the act of firing shall both lock the breechpiece and fire the charge.

It also consists in the construction and use of the globular surface on the front end of the movable breechpiece, in combination with the cylindrical cartridge-case, for the purpose of more effectually preventing the escape of gas at the joint.

It also consists in the construction and use of the lever, substantially as described, for the purpose of retracting the cartridge-case from the barrel.'[7]

The patent reads:

'I claim —

1. The percussion-rod in a movable breechpiece, in combination with the sliding bolt, when so arranged that the lock in the act of firing shall both make fast the breechpiece and

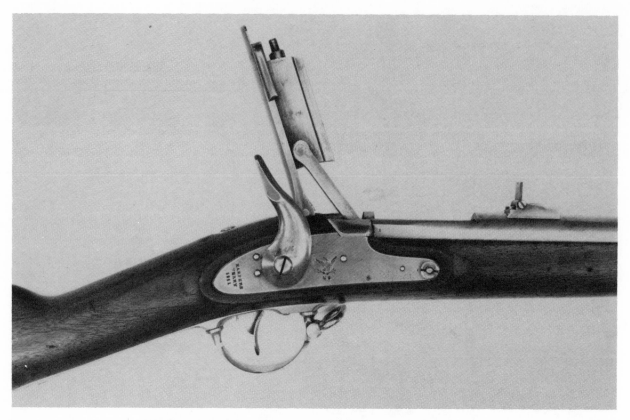

The action of the Morse conversion Model 1841 rifle shown open for loading.

fire the charge.

2. The construction and use of the globular surface on the front end of the movable breechpiece, in combination with the end of the cylindrical cartridge-case, for the purpose of more effectually preventing the escape of gas at the joint.

3. The construction and use of the lever, when arranged substantially as described, for the purpose of retracting the cartridge-case.'[8]

What made Morse's breech-loading design so favorable was the centerfire cartridge used in these arms. The same day that he received his breech-loading patent, October 28, 1856, Morse was issued U. S. Patent No. 15,996 for his cartridge cases. His letters patent claim read:

'The combination and arrangement of the cartridge case, as constructed, with the priming appartus, as constructed, or their equivalents, whereby I effect the entire exclusion of any and all escape of the gas produced by the combustion of the powder of the cartridge and priming, except by the one channel--the bore of the barrel of the gun — the breech-joints and priming-vent

being thereby so effectually sealed and closed that no air can escape at these parts of the gun after the charge is fired until the cartridge-case is withdrawn from the bore, although air blown in at the muzzle before firing the charge might escape through these joints, as it would in the cases above referred to.'[9]

As previously stated, these .69 caliber centerfire cartridges used in the Morse alterations were the first centerfire arms manufactured by the National Armories.

The Morse system required machining out a section of the breech and installing the pivoting-type breechblock. The nipple was removed and the top portion of the bolster was machined off. The front section of the hammer was cut away — the function of the hammer was to serve as a locking device for the breech-block. At half cock the breechblock can be manually raised up and back to insert the .69 caliber centerfire cartridge. Squeezing the trigger drops the hammer and drives the locking bolt forward. This motion in turn strikes the firing pin sending it forward to strike the cartridge.

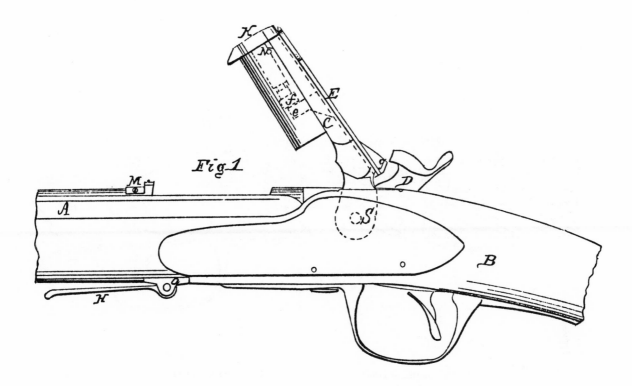

The drawings attached to G.W. Morse's Patent No. 20,503 of June 8, 1858 illustrating his breech mechanism.

In March of 1857, Morse first had his design tested by the Ordnance Department with favorable results. Later, in November 1857, the Navy test fired the Morse at the Washington Navy Yard. Captain Ingraham, Chief of Naval Ordnance at the Washington Navy Yard, was informed by the testing officers that on November 9 and 10 the Morse was fired one hundred five times with excellent results. The arm was an admirable breechloader because it:

1. Had a moderate recoil.

2. The ammunition placed in water would not destroy its effectiveness.

3. Bore did not lead up.

4. The machinery of the piece performed its functions perfectly well under the serve test to which it was subjected.[10]

With these favorable test results, Secretary of War John Floyd ordered, on March 5, 1858, that one hundred Morse guns be purchased at $40 each and be paid for in lots of twenty-five each as soon as inspected and delivered. No arms, however, appear to ever have been delivered as a result of this order.

On July 8, 1858, John Floyd appointed a board to proceed to West Point to examine all methods of altering to breechloading and report upon the adoptability of each method in the alteration of muzzleloading arms. The board met at West Point on July 22 and upon completion of their test trials found in favor of the Morse design and its new centerfire cartridge. The board recommended that a number of old United States muskets be altered to the Morse pattern and be adopted for field trials by troops in service.

With the board's approval of his design, George Morse on September 9, 1858 offered to allow the Government to alter two thousand five hundred of their old arms to his design for the sum of $5 each. The Secretary of War accepted this proposal to the extent of two thousand arms and the sum of $10,000 was paid to Morse. On November 6 and 9, 1858, orders were given to the superintendent at Springfield Armory to begin the alterations to the Morse pattern. On June 28, 1859, Morse made further modifications in his alteration which were

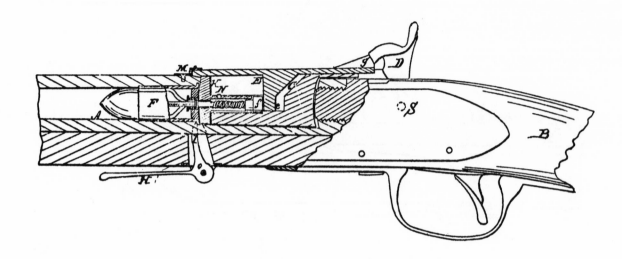

The drawing attached to Edward Linder's 1859 Patent No. 23,378.

accepted by the Ordnance Department with expressed conditions that all work on this alteration would cease as soon as $4,200 was spent regardless of how many or how few arms were altered. The superintendent at Springfield on November 12 reported that the $4,200 had been spent with fifty-four arms having been completed and another five hundred forty arms in various stages of completion. These fifty-four altered muskets were sent to the Washington Arsenal. In July of 1860, orders were received from the Secretary of War that a model rifle, tools, gauges and mills suited for the Morse alteration be sent from Springfield to the Harpers Ferry Arsenal for the purpose of altering the 1841 .54 caliber rifles. On July 19, 1860 these items were received at Harpers Ferry and were being manufactured at the arsenal at the time of its capture by the Confederates in April of 1861.

During the Civil War, the Morse inventions were stored away at the Springfield Armory and Frankford and Washington Arsenals. George Morse on the other hand cast his lot with the Confederacy and in Greenville, South Carolina manufactured carbines for the

state militia of South Carolina. These carbines were manufactured on machinery which had been captured by the Confederates from the Harpers Ferry Armory.

In 1875, Morse attempted to collect royalties from the Government for each breech-loading arm manufactured by the Government claiming patent infringement. In this suit, he was completely unsuccessful.

Of the approximately six hundred fifty-five arms altered to the Morse design, most were altered from the .69 caliber 1816 musket and the .54 caliber Model 1841 Harpers Ferry rifles. How the Government disposed of these arms in the post war years is uncertain, however, there is record of one Morse rifle being sold by the Ordnance office for five dollars to Francis Bannerman on May 16, 1881.[11]

LINDNER

The Lindner system of alteration to breech-loading consisted of cutting of the barrel about four and one-half inches from the breech and inserting a pivoting breech section complete with nipple bolster. A bolt operating sleeve for-

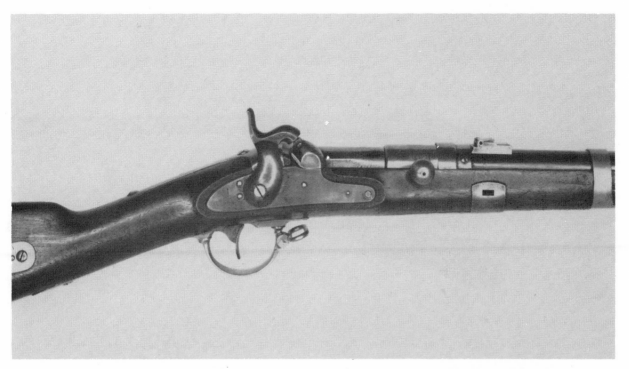

One of the 100 Model 1841 rifles altered to the Lindner breech loading system by the State of Massachusetts late in 1861. The conversion was carried out by Allen & Morse of Boston.   — Milwaukee Public Museum collection

ward of the breech is turned to the left which allows the breechblock to spring upward similar to the Hall for inserting a .54 caliber combustible cartridge. The breechblock is then firmly pressed down and the locking collar is turned to the right for closing. In addition, these rifles were given a new longer barrel tang and reinforcing floor plate for extra strength plus a new rear sight graduated to five hundred yards and a bayonet stud-blade front sight.

This alteration was the invention of Edward Lindner of New York City having received his U.S. Patent No. 23,378 on March 29, 1859. His patent claim read:

'What I claim as new, and desire to secure by Letters Patent, is —

1. The method herein described for operating or closing the breech, and forming a tight joint at the junction of the barrel with the breech, by the employment of a screw ferrule or sleeve fitting an outer screw-thread on the barrel, and provided with a projecting annular-flange for grasping and releasing the breech, and for drawing the same backward and forward in the direction of the barrel to or from the rear end thereof upon said screw-threaded sleeve, being

operated substantially as herein described.

2. In combination with a movable box within the breech, constructed and operating as described, the packing thereof by means of asbestos or its equivalent, substantially in the manner and for the purposes described.

3. Locking the screw-threaded sleeve that operates the breech by forming the pivoted lever, which serves to turn said sleeve, with an eccentric or cam arranged to act upon a locking-pin by pressing down said lever after the breech is drawn tight, as herein set forth.'[12]

The Lindner alterations were not performed at the National Armories but were the result of the State of Massachusetts decision to alter one hundred .54 caliber Model 1841 rifles to this system. In late 1861, the Master of Ordnance for the State of Massachusetts entered into a contract with Allen and Morse of Boston to alter one hundred Model 1841 rifles manufactured by Robbins and Lawrence of Windsor, Vermont. In 1862, Enos G. Allen was paid $1,125.50 for these alterations plus $7.50 for three bayonets and scabbards.[13] A.J. Drake of Boston was paid to clean these rifles and add new front and rear sights. In addition three rifles were altered by

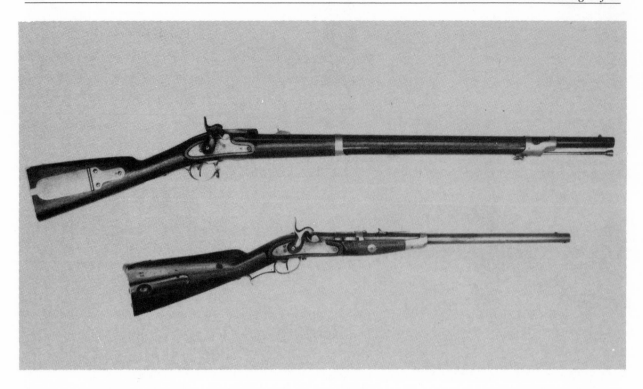

(top) Another Model 1841 rifle — this one altered to the Merrill breechloading system. (bottom) An Austrian carbine altered to the Lindner system. Austria was the only country to officially adopt this breechloader conversion.   — Milwaukee Public Museum collection

the Amoskeag Manufacturing Company of Manchester, New Hampshire. All one hundred three of these altered Lindner rifles remained in the State armory at Cambridge throughout the war and finally were sold at public auction in 1865.

MERRILL

James H. Merrill's method of alteration to breechloading was covered by U.S. Patent No. 20,954 of July 20, 1858. This patent was taken out to cover the alteration of Jenks carbines to his breech-loading design so that the Jenks could use combustible cartridges instead of loose powder and ball. Merrill's method of alteration was to replace the original tang/-breech plug with the Merrill breech mechanism including attaching a latch for the lever on top of the barrel. A clean-out screw to the original nipple bolster and a reinforcing screw to the lockplate were also added.

On April 19, 1859, Merrill, Latrobe and Thomas entered into a contract with the Ordnance Department 'to alter 100 rifled percussion musket caliber .69, 100 percussion rifles reamed out caliber .58 and 100 rifled musketoons at $10

each.'[14] By September 19, 1860, they had delivered ninety-six muskets (Model 1842), ninety-eight musketoons and eighty-six rifles (Model 1841). About three hundred arms were altered by Merrill, Latrobe and Thomas plus two hundred forty Jenks carbines.

The bullets used in these converted arms were a 0.58 inch diameter bullet weighing four hundred fifty grains with fifty grams of powder for the 58 caliber Merrills; and a 0.69 inch diameter bullet weighing seven hundred twenty grains with sixty - seventy grains of powder for the 69 caliber Model 1842 muskets.

In June of 1860, Major R. E. Colston of Virginia Military Institute (VMI) test fired a number of breech-loading arms for possible state purchase and had this to say in his report of June 28:

'MERRILL'S Breech-Loading Arms — MR. Merrill claims no other advantage for his arms than the method of breech-loading. This may be applied to any barrels. Among the arms submitted, are a U.S. musket and a U.S. Harper's Ferry Rifle altered to breech-loading by this process.

I have no hesitation in saying, that of all the

breech-loading arms I have seen, these seem to me the best suited for the purposes we have in view, and for the following reasons:

SOLIDITY — Merrill's arrangement seems to offer great strength, and to be able to stand heavy charges. There does not seem to be any friction between the parts, which can lead to rapid wearing.

SIMPLICITY — The breech-loading apparatus is very simple, and easy to take to pieces and put together again for cleaning or oiling. I have not been able to detect any escape of gas.

AMMUNITION — The great advantage of these arms over the others is, that they can be used with the paper cartridge or with loose powder and ball, without any metallic or other cartridge case. This secures one of the indispensible conditions of an arm of war.

Another advantage of Mr. Merrill's patent is the ease with which it may be applied to other arms. Take for example the U.S. Minnie rifle altered by him. It has the same barrel, stock and lock. Nothing is removed but the old breech screw, and the arm is not in the least degree diminished in solidity, and hardly changed at all in appearance. It must be added to this, that this altered arm seemed to have the same range and force with 50 grains of powder as the unaltered rifle with the regular charge of sixty grains.

If it should be thought adviseable to give breech-loading carbines to cavalry, and breech-loading muskets and rifles to the sergeants of infantry, I would give the preference, so far as I am able to judge, to Mr. Merrill's arms.'[15]

The number of Merrill rifles used by the Confederates during the war is unknown, however, the lst Virginia Cavalry was armed with the Merrill carbine.

It appears that the altered Merrill's remained in the Northern Arsenals throughout the war and saw no military use. As of December 31, 1862, eighty-six of the .58 caliber Merrill altered rifles were in storage at the Washington Arsenal.[16] Many of these rifles were in Government storage for many years after the Civil War. As late as the third quarter of 1883, the New York City Arsenal sold ninety-two altered .69 caliber Merrills for a total sales price of $79 or 85 cents each.[17] As late as January 2, 1895, twenty of the .58 caliber Merrills were sold to L.E. Lumbert for $1.50 each.[18]

For additional details concerning the Merrill arms, see descriptions and illustrations in chapter eight.

[1]U.S. Patent Office, U.S. Patent No. 15,307 dated July 8, 1856.
[2]Edward A. Hull, *Mont Storm Civil War Carbines,* Man At Arms, July/August 1981, p. 38.
[3]NARG 74-145.
[4]Ibid.
[5]Ibid.
[6]U.S. Patent Office, U.S. Patent No. 15,995 dated October 28, 1856.
[7]U.S. Patent Office, U.S. Patent No. 20,503 dated June 8, 1858.
[8]Ibid.
[9]U.S. Patent Office, U.S. Patent No. 15,996, dated October 28, 1856.
[10]NARG 74-145.
[11]NARG 156-125.
[12]U.S. Patent Office, U.S. Patent No. 23,378 dated March 29, 1859.
[13]Public Document No. 7, State of Massachusetts, Report of Master of Ordnance 1862, P. 7 and 11.
[14]NARG 156-152.
[15]L.D. Satterlee, *The Merrill Rifle,* 10 Old Gun Cataogs, Chicago: 1962, p. 15 and 16.
[16]NARG 156-101.
[17]NARG 156-125.
[18]NARG 156-124.

BIBLIOGRAPHY

Printed Books and Pamphlets

Annual Report, the Quartermaster General to the Governor of the State of Kentucky for the 1863-4, Frankfort: 1865.

Benedict, G.G., *Vermont in the Civil War, 2 Vols.*, Burlington: 1888.

Battles and Leaders of the Civil War, New York: 1956.

Brown, S.E. Jr., *The Guns of Harpers Ferry*, Berrysville: 1968.

Dyer, F.H., *A Compendium of the War of the Rebellion*, Dayton: 1978.

Edwards, W.B., *Civil War Guns*, Harrisburg: 1962.

Executive Document. No. 99, 40th Congress, 2nd Session, 1868.

Executive Document No. 16-2, 39th Congress.

Flayderman, N., *Flayderman's Guide to Antique American Firearms and their Values*, Northfield: 1977.

Fuller, C.E., *The Breech-Loader in the Service 1816-1917*, New Milford: 1965.

Gardner, Col. R.E., *Small Arms Makers*: 1963.

Gluckman, A., *Identifying Old U.S. Muskets, Rifles and Carbines*, New York: 1965.

Hale, L.V. and Phillips, S.S., *History of the 49th Virginia Infantry c.s.a.*, Lanham: 1981.

Hicks, J.E., *U.S. Military Firearms*, Alhambra: 1962.

Heitman, F.B., *Historical Register and Dictionary of the United States Army from its Organization September 29, 1789 to March 2, 1903*, Washington: 1903.

Higginson, T.W., *Massachusetts in the Army and Navy During the War 1861-1865*, Boston: 1895.

Huntington, R.T., *Halls Breechloaders*, York: 1972.

Hopkins, R.E., *Military Sharps Rifles and Carbines Volume I*, San Jose: 1967.

Joint Committee on the Conduct of the War - Congressional Serial Set No. 1142, 1862.

Lewis, Col. B.R., *Notes on Ammunition of the American Civil War*, Washington: 1959.

Lewis, W.T., *C.M. Spencer:The Man and His Inventions*, American Society of Arms Collectors, October: 1978.

Lord, F.A., *They Fought For the Union*, Harrisburg: 1960.

McAulay, J.D., *Carbines of the Civil War 1861-1865*, Union City: 1981.

Minnigh, L.W., *Gettysburg What They Did Here*, Gettysburg: 1954.

Official Records of the Rebellion, GPO: 1891.

Partial Roster of the Survivors of Berdan's U.S. Sharpshooters First and Second Regiments 1861-1865, Washington, D.C.: 1889.

Public Document No. 7 *State of Massachusetts, Report of Master Of Ordnance*: Boston: 1862.

Reilly, R.M., *United States Military Small Arms 1816-1865*, Baton Rouge: 1970.

Ripley, Wm. Y. Lt. Col., *Vermont Riflemen in the War for the Union, 1861-1865 - A History of Company 'F' First United States Sharpshooters*, Rutland: 1883.

Roe, A.S., *The Fifth Massachusetts Infantry*, Boston: 1911.

Satterlee, L.D., *10 Old Gun Catalogs*, Chicago: 1962.

Sellers, F., *Sharps Firearms* North Hollywood: 1978.

Sheridan, P.H., *Personal Memories of P.H. Sheridan*, New York: 1888.

Stevens, C.A., Capt., *Berdan's U.S. Sharpshooters in the Army of the Potomac*, Dayton: 1972.

Thomas, D.S., *Ready Aim Fire*, Biglerville: 1981.

Todd, F.P., *American Military Equipaqe 1851-1872 Vol. II State Forces*, Chatham Squire Press, Inc.: 1983.

National Archives

RECORDS OF THE BUREAU OF ORDNANCE, RECORD GROUP 74.

Section 3. Letters Sent to Navy Yards and Stations 1842-84.
         5. Misc. Letters Sent 1842-83.
         6. Letters and Telegrams Sent 1861-1911.
        22. Misc. Letters Received 1842-84.
       101. Reports of Target Practice With Small Arms 1868.

       157. Record of Contracts 1842-62.
       158. Record of Accounts Approved For Payment 1842-1903.
       165. Record of Ordnance Contracts for 1861.
       145. Correspondence Regarding The Examination of Inventions 1851-80.

REGIMENTAL AND COMPANY ORDER AND LETTER BOOKS, RECORD GROUP 94. lst U.S. SHARPSHOOTERS.

RECORDS OF THE CHIEF OF ORDNANCE, RECORD GROUP 156.

Section 7. Letters, Endorsements and Telegrams Sent.
        79. Purchases of Ordnance 1861-67.
        81. Contracts and Orders for Ordnance 1861-97.
       100. Quarterly Statements of Ordnance on Hand at Forts 1862-64.
       101. Quarterly Statements of Ordnance on Hand at Arsenals and Depots 1862-63.
       108. Inventories of Ordnance as of October 24, 1862.
       110. Quarterly Statement of Ordnance in Cavalry 1862-64.
       111. Quarterly Statement of Ordnance in Infantry 1862-71.

       118. Ordnance issued to the Militia 1816-1904.
       124. Sales of Ordnance at Depots and Arsenals 1864-1907.
       125. Sales of Ordnance at Depots and Arsenals 1865-94.
       152. Statements of Accounts for Contractors 1817-1905.
       164. Accounts Sent to the Second Auditor 1861-79.
       201. Report of Experiments 1826-71.
       215. Abstracts of Army Officers Reports on Small Arms 1863-64
       994. Correspondence Relating to Inventions 1812-70.
      1001. Correspondence and Reports Relating to Experiments 1818-70.

Magazine Articles

Austerman, W.R., *The Spencer in Confederate Service*, Arms Gazette, Sept. 1980.

_____ *Virginia Cavalcade*, Winter 1985.

Albaugh, W.A. III, *Union Armament in the Civil War*, North South Trader, March/April 1975.

Arnold, R.E., *The Jenks Breechloaders*, Man At Arms, Nov./Dec. 1980.

Davis, R.V., *The Spencer Navy Rifle*, Gun Report, August 1874.

Dorsey, R.S., *The Colt Revolving Shotgun*, The Gun Report, Dec. 1975

Fairbain, C.J. & Patterson, C.M., *Captain Hall, Inventor*, The Gun Report, October & November 1959.

Gussman, R.A. & Lindsay, R.E., *Spencer Repeating Rifle Company*, Gun Report, January 1967.

Harrower, G. Jr., *N-SSA Teams Then and Now - 2nd New Jersey Volunteer Infantry*, The Skirmish Line, March-April 1981.

Hull, E.A., *Mont Storm Civil War Carbines*, Man At Arms, July/August 1981.

_____ *Ballard 'Old Model' Firearms*, The Gun Report, June/July 1985.

Harpers Weekly, February 11, 1865.

Lustyik, A.F., *The Breechloaders of James Durell Greene, Gun Report*, November/December 1971 and January 1972.

_____ *The Jenks Carbine (Part 2)*, Gun Report, August 1964.

_____ *The Joslyn Carbine*, Gun Report, Sept. and Oct. 1962.

Lindert, A.W., *Sharps Rifles for the USN*, Gun Report, September 1979.

Marcot, R.M., *Springfield Armory Conversions and Repairs to Spencer Repeating carbines*, Gun Report, July 1980.

_____ *The Blakeslee 'Quick-Loader'*, Man At Arms, March/April 1982.

_____ *Christopher Spencer's Yankee Lighting*, America, The Men and Their Guns That Made Her Great, Los Angeles 1981.

McAulay, J.D., *Spencer Rifles for Wilder's Brigade at Chickagauqa*, Gun Report, January 1980.

_____ *The Greene Rifle*, Gun Report, February 1981.

_____ *Breech Loading Carbines for Lincoln's Cavalry*, The Gun Report, April 1980.

Nehrbass, A.F., *The Springfield Joslyn Rifle*, The American Rifleman, December 1972.

Osborn, A.F., *The Merrill Rifle*, Gun Report, April 1958.

_____ *More on the Merrill Rifle*, Gun Report, July 1959.

Salzer, J.R., *The Sharps & Hankins Carbine*, Gun Report, January 1963.

Sword, W., *The Berdan Sharps Rifles*, Man At Arms, May/June 1979

_____ *The Berdan Sharps Rifle An Update*, Man At Arms, July/Aug. 1980.

Vinovich, R.M., *The Man Behind Colt, Elisha King Root*, Gun Report October 1970.